SACRED FEASTS

FROM A MONASTERY KITCHEN

RECIPES and REFLECTIONS

From the Best-Selling Author of
From a Monastery Kitchen

Brother Victor-Antoine d'Avila-Latourrette

Liguori
LIGUORI, MISSOURI

Imprimi Potest:
Thomas D. Picton, C.Ss.R.
Provincial, Denver Province
The Redemptorists

Published by Liguori Publications
Liguori, Missouri 63057-9999

Library of Congress Cataloging-in-Publication Data
D'Avila-Latourrette, Victor-Antoine.
    Sacred feasts : from a monastery kitchen / Victor-Antoine d'Avila-Latourrette.
       p. cm.
    ISBN 978-0-7648-1862-2
    1. Vegetarian cookery. 2. Church year meditations. 3. Cookery—Religious aspects—Christianity. I. Title.

    TX837.D234 2009
    641.5'636—dc22

                             2009019992

A French-language softcover edition of this English work by Victor-Antoine D'Avila-Latourrette was published in 2007 by Les Éditions de l'Homme under the title *Dans la cuisine du frère Victor-Antoine: Réflexions et recettes inspirées par les saisons.*

Scripture citations are taken from the *New Revised Standard Version* of the Bible, copyright 1989 by the Division of Christian Education of the National Council of Churches of Christ in the USA. All rights reserved. Used with permission.

Liguori Publications, a nonprofit corporation, is an apostolate of the Redemptorists. To learn more about the Redemptorists, visit Redemptorists.com.

To order, call 800-325-9521.
www.liguori.org

Printed in the United States of America
13 12 11 10 09   5 4 3 2 1
First edition

Contents

NOVEMBER

DECEMBER

Introduction

LIFE IN A MONASTERY KITCHEN has a unique appeal. After my monastic-themed cookbooks *From a Monastery Kitchen* and *Twelve Months of Monastery Soups* were published, readers asked for more daily moments, happenings, inspirations, and anecdotes from our monastic kitchen. Those requests gave birth to the idea of a book that shares the intimate workings of a monastery kitchen, which in many ways is no different than that of an ordinary home.

Each chapter conveys a vision and approach to food spirituality that underscore the sacred place meals have in a monastery. To the monk cook, food is sacred because God created it and because Jesus gave himself under its auspices. It's little wonder the monks of old described their reverent approach to food as the "sacrament of the table."

Sacred Feasts closely follows the secular and monastic calendars, including Christmas, New Year's Day, Easter, Pentecost, Memorial Day, Fourth of July, Labor Day, and Thanksgiving as well as times that call for more sobriety and restraint, such as Lent and Advent. Mother Nature's calendar also profoundly influences the day-to-day events in any monastery. This is particularly true in our monastery because of its location in the New York–New England border, where the four seasons are lived in all their plenitude.

I composed the essays and prepared the menus on the dates given at the beginning of the essays, at least six per month. The essays begin with an inspirational quotation, relate the weather and particulars of the day, continue with the work in the kitchen and gardens, describe the day's feast or event, and conclude with the day's menu. Some of the recipes are provided so readers can recreate and experiment with the dishes, authentic food both for the body and the soul.

I hope readers are inspired by these candid kitchen tales and discover in themselves an affinity for the monastic approach to cooking, which is characterized by simplicity, tastefulness, and resilient frugality. It's also imbued with the innumerable joys and ways of praising God daily through the practice of food spirituality in the humble sanctuary of the kitchen.

Bon appétit à tous!

BROTHER VICTOR-ANTOINE D'AVILA-LATOURRETTE
FEAST OF PENTECOST, 2009

Let us strive to make the present moment beautiful.

SAINT FRANCIS DE SALES

Measurement–Conversion Chart

United States Customary Unit Equivalents

1 pinch = $\frac{1}{16}$ teaspoon

1 dash = $\frac{1}{8}$ teaspoon

3 teaspoons = 1 tablespoon

4 tablespoons = ¼ cup

48 teaspoons = 1 cup

16 tablespoons = 1 cup

2 cups = 1 pint

2 pints = 1 quart

4 quarts = 1 gallon

8 fluid ounces = 1 cup

16 dry ounces = 1 pound

United States Customary Units to Metric Units

1 teaspoon = 5 milliliters

1 tablespoon = 15 milliliters

1 cup = 240 milliliters

1 pint = 470 milliliters

1 quart = .95 liter

1 gallon = 3.8 liters

1 fluid ounce = 30 milliliters

1 dry ounce = 28 grams

1 pound = 454 grams

JANUARY

*J*ANUARY is the birth month of the year. Once more we complete another full life cycle as we say goodbye to the old year, and then suddenly we're face-to-face with the new. What will the new year bring, we all ask? What surprises does it have in store? We enter into something new, and it inescapably makes us wonder about its unpredictability, its possible surprises, its uncertain future, its final purpose, and its eventual outcome.

Today is also the feast of Mary, the Mother of God. Whatever the year has in store, it's a good omen that we begin its counting under her unfailing protection. Mary reminds us that all time is God's time; we must not cling to it as a possession, but as something to use wisely during our earthly life just as she and Christ did during their time on Earth. As we begin the new year, it's good to seriously consider how we use the length of time given to us, how we spend our days, and what our ultimate goals are. So New Year's Day is not only an occasion for celebration, but also for serious reflection on the purpose of our lives and for resolutions on enhancing our future days and making them richer with gifts from the Spirit of God.

Since just before Christmas Day—over a week now—our monastery kitchen has been busy with festal table preparations as the celebration of the Lord's Incarnation is expressed in our food arrangements. Today, in spite of its being New Year's Day and the solemnity of the Mother of God, I decided I needed contrast to our festive meals of the last few days. I'm deliberately celebrating with food of rustic origins, hearty and soul-warming, just what we need to face the cold temperatures. Rustic meals have a charm and refinement all their own. There's something so friendly, so simple and earthy, about them. They're not fancy, but they are appetizing and delicious, they easily warm our hearts, and they go a long way toward inspiring conviviality at a gathering.

Today's meal consists of a hearty hot soup that can be started the day before, a cheese

*January,
the first month
of the year,
like its namesake,
looks back
over the past,
and forward
to the future,
with hope and
good resolutions.*

ANONYMOUS

fondue, a mixed-green salad, and a plain flan for dessert. Fondue's communal nature as a meal makes it an appealing and irresistible dish, so appropriate for New Year's Day. Besides, it's easy, economical, and fun to share with friends.

All in all, this rustic holiday meal—a mirror of our simple lifestyle—has nothing to envy of more sumptuous celebrations. The soup and the dessert, though not elaborate, take a bit more time and can be prepared a day ahead; in fact, the soup usually tastes better the next day. The fondue and the salad demand less time and can be done on the same day.

PASTA E FAGIOLI SOUP (Bean and Pasta Soup)
6–8 SERVINGS

1 pound dried white navy beans
8 cups cold water
3 leeks, trimmed at the top, thinly sliced
2 potatoes, peeled and cubed
1 large carrot, peeled and cubed
1 celery stalk, thinly sliced
1 tablespoon fresh or dried rosemary
1 tablespoon fresh or dried thyme
2 cups Italian dry white wine
Sea salt and freshly ground pepper
1 cup small macaroni or other tubular pasta
5 tablespoons extra-virgin olive oil

1 Place beans and water in a large soup pot and soak overnight, covered, for 10 to 12 hours. The next day add vegetables, rosemary, thyme, and wine. Bring soup to a boil, then lower heat to medium. Cook slowly for about 2 hours. Cover. Add more water if necessary.

2 Using a ladle, set aside 1 cup of the bean-vegetables mixture. Also set aside separately 2 cups of the liquid.

3 Make sure there is sufficient liquid in the soup. Just before ready to serve, add pasta and simmer over low heat until pasta is cooked. Stir frequently.

4 Place in a blender the cup of bean-vegetable mixture, the 2 cups of liquid, and the olive oil and blend thoroughly. When pasta is cooked, add this mixture. Reheat a bit and serve hot.

After the hearty bean and pasta soup, serve the fondue and basic mixed salad. Fondue is a marvelous dish to serve on a special occasion such as New Year's Day, when friends can gather informally around the fireplace and share something delicious in an intimate setting. There's nothing like shared food to enhance the moment and the pleasure of the company.

CHEESE FONDUE

6–8 SERVINGS

2 garlic cloves
2½ cups dry white wine
2 cups grated Gruyère cheese
2 cups Swiss, or other cheese
3 tablespoons French brandy
1 tablespoon cornstarch
Sea salt and freshly ground pepper
Pinch of nutmeg
1 crusty French baguette cut into
  bite-size pieces (warm in oven
  if necessary)

1 Crush garlic cloves and rub them on the surface of a medium-size iron pot or fondue pot. Pour wine into the pot, add cheese, and stir continuously over medium heat until cheese melts.

2 Mix brandy and cornstarch into a paste and add to cheese mixture. Continue stirring until the mixture achieves a creamy consistency. Season to taste with salt, pepper, and nutmeg. Stir well for several minutes. Place fondue pot over a wood stove or fondue flame and let your family and friends dip their bread with long forks into the fondue mixture. Accompany the fondue with a mixed-green salad.

BASIC MIXED SALAD

6–8 SERVINGS

1 head frisée (French curly endive), trimmed
1 bunch fresh watercress, trimmed with stems discarded
2 Belgian endives, leaves separated and halved lengthwise
1 small red onion, thinly sliced

VINAIGRETTE
5 tablespoons extra-virgin olive oil
2 tablespoons red-wine vinegar
Salt and freshly ground pepper

1 Place salad greens in a large salad bowl. Just before serving, drizzle olive oil on top.

2 Toss to coat. Add vinegar, salt, and pepper to taste. Toss once more and serve.

FLAN A L'ANCIENNE (Flan Old-Fashioned Style)

8 SERVINGS

2½ cups milk

1 vanilla bean,
   split lengthwise

½ cup sugar (taste and
   add more if needed)

3 large eggs

2 egg yolks

½ cup sweetened
   condensed milk

4 tablespoons sugar

1 tablespoon French brandy

1 Preheat oven to 350° F.

2 Heat milk in a medium-size pot over medium flame. Add vanilla-bean halves and stir until milk turns hot. Remove pot from heat, set it aside, and cover for 30 minutes.

3 Dissolve sugar in a medium-size nonstick skillet over low-medium heat, moving and shaking skillet to help sugar melt evenly. Continue cooking and stirring sugar until it melts and turns deep brown. Immediately pour dissolved sugar into 8 small ramekins (about 6-ounce custard bowls). Tilt each bowl to coat the bottom thoroughly. Let cool.

4 With a mixer, combine eggs, egg yolks, condensed milk, sugar, and brandy until mixture is perfectly smooth. Remove and discard vanilla bean; gradually whisk egg mixture into milk.

5 Pour the custard mixture into the ramekins. Divide evenly. Place the ramekins into a large oven pan with water covering the bottom half of the ramekins (*bain marie,* "water bath"). Place the pan in the oven with a sheet of foil covering the top of the ramekins. Cook the flan for about 30 to 40 minutes until done. Check its consistency with a thin knife or pin before removing the flan from the oven.

6 When done, remove the ramekins from the oven and allow the flan to cool over a rack. Chill for 2 hours, and then unmold the flan by carefully running a thin knife around the edges of the flan. When the flan feels loose, with great care turn each ramekin upside down onto a serving plate, release the flan, and serve.

Hunger and thirst,

O Christ,

for sight of thee,

Thou sole

provision for the

unknown way.

Long hunger

wasted for the

world wanderer,

With sight of thee

may he be

satisfied.

RADBOD OF UTRECHT

(C. 900)

T'S BEEN an extraordinarily cold winter. "What else is new?" some of my neighbors would say. But we've already had a series of steady snow-storms, and it's only early January!

The winter air is perfectly still, and the gift from the heavens will be here a long, long time. Northeasterners get used to being shut in by the snow because the roads and trails that connect us to the outside world are closed. Outdoors, beyond the monastery, all nature is silent and white and clean. I thank God for the bright fire from the wood stove in our kitchen. The warmth it radiates is such a comfort on days like today.

Today is Epiphany, the twelfth day after Christmas. This beautiful feast reminds us of the manifestation of God in the world. On Christmas Day the goodness of God became visible to our very eyes in the form of a baby, in the revealed humanity of Christ, the Son of God and sole image of the eternal Father. The Incarnation of the Son of God and his earthly appearance in our midst changed the course of human history—of humanity—to whom he came as a savior.

In the Latin Mediterranean countries, today's feast is commonly known as the Feast of the Three Kings after today's Gospel reading, the story of the three Magi. Guided by a mysterious star, they came from afar to the Bethlehem grotto to pay homage to the tiny child, the King of Kings.

Many customs, varying from country to country and from monastery to mon-astery, are associated with this lovely feast. In France, one beautiful ancient custom that survives is the preparation of the *gateau des rois*, "cake of the kings." A piece of cake set aside for the infant Jesus is given to the first poor person who knocks at the door asking for food. An important aspect of this charming ritual is the search for a small fava bean hidden in the cake. The person who prepares the cake places a small bean in it. The person who finds the bean is declared king or queen for a day. Those present toast the king/queen, in France with a sweet dessert wine like a Muscadet; the king/queen then moves to the head of the table.

Many recipes exist for the *gateau des rois*; every region or corner of France has its favorite. The following recipe, in my view, is the least time-consuming. A friend from Belgium received the recipe from a great aunt in northern France. I've simpli-fied it and brought it to contemporary standards of baking. In many ways, the recipe isn't much different from our own *gateau* from the Pyrenees.

GATEAU DES ROIS (Three Kings' Day Cake)

10–12 SERVINGS

1 packet dry yeast
½ teaspoon sugar
¼ cup sugar
1 cup milk, boiled and
    then cooled to
    lukewarm temperature
4½ cups all-purpose flour
¼ teaspoon salt
3 tablespoons cognac
1 stick unsalted butter,
    cut into small pieces
4 egg yolks
1 dried fava bean or
    pecan nut

ICING

2 sticks sweet butter
¾ cup granulated sugar
1 tablespoon cognac
1 teaspoon vanilla extract

1 Butter well an 11½ by 16-inch cake pan.

2 Empty yeast packet into warm milk, add ½ teaspoon sugar, and stir well. Let stand for about 5 minutes or until it foams.

3 Combine in a large bowl flour, salt, cognac, remaining sugar, butter pieces, egg yolks, and yeast mixture. Mix ingredients by hand or mixer until the liquid is absorbed by the flour. Remove dough from bowl and place it on a large, floured surface.

4 Add fava bean or a whole pecan nut (your choice) to the dough and begin kneading the dough back and forth for about 15 minutes or until it turns evenly smooth. If necessary, sprinkle dough with extra flour so it doesn't stick to the work surface.

5 Carefully arrange dough in a buttered bowl and turn both sides so they're evenly coated with butter. Cover dough with a clean towel and let rise for 1 hour or until it doubles in size.

6 After dough rises, punch it down in the bowl and coat it with butter as before. Cover dough with towel and let it rise until it doubles in size.

7 Move dough from the bowl to the work surface and press it flat with your hands. Raise dough with your hands and place it carefully into buttered cake pan. Press it with your fingers into sides and corners. Cover dough with towel and let it rise for about 1 hour or until it doubles in size. Preheat oven to 375° F.

8 Prepare icing: Mix butter, sugar, cognac, and vanilla in a small bowl. Blend thoroughly and set aside.

9 Using your fingers, make small indentations throughout the surface of the dough. Use a spatula to distribute the icing evenly over the surface of the dough. Place cake pan in the middle of the oven and bake for about 40 minutes or until sugar–butter mixture turns gold. Remove from oven and let it cool on a wire rack. At dessert time, place the cake at the center of the table.

THIS MORNING I arose a bit later than usual. While opening the porch door to let out our dog and cats, I realized the temperature was well below zero. The sun was shining and the sky was pale blue, but the brutally cold wind conveyed an air of gloom. This is January, after all. Mother Nature never lies: We hear her speak though symbols and signs, but her language and message is always clear and concise. I breathed the winter air deeply before closing the door, and instantly I recognized that unmistakable New York–New England air unique to our region. Our wintry air is undeniably fierce, cold, and at times savage, but it's also dry and clear and sometimes as soothing as a tonic. People who live in the countryside develop an awareness of these subtle daily changes in the air.

Today is the feast of the Theophany of the Lord, the feast that concludes and closes the Christmas cycle. It commemorates the manifestation of the divine Trinity during the moment of Christ's baptism in the Jordan. It's an unusual event: As Christ humbles himself seeking baptism from John, the Spirit descends upon him and the voice of the Father expresses his pleasure with his only son. For the first time, the three divine persons of the Trinity are visibly revealed in the New Testament. It's truly an ineffable mystery, the kind of mystery that encompasses and demands our entire assent and faith. God is so great, so transcendent, so beyond us—yet at the same time, through his becoming flesh and one of us, he is so very close to us.

Since the temperature is so cold and today's feast calls for something special, I decided yesterday that our soup of the day would be an unusual one not often made here and that won't be taken for granted by those who share it. It's much loved in the Mediterranean world and is made basically made of freshly roasted chestnuts. On a cold night, nothing beats the fragrance of freshly roasted chestnuts transformed into a delicious, hearty soup, the kind of soup that lingers for days in the memory of those who share it.

The appreciation of chestnuts is not so evident in American kitchens as it is in Europe. Perhaps it's a question of custom and tradition. It could also be because chestnut trees aren't as abundant in the United States as in Europe: Most of the chestnuts available in American supermarkets are imported from Italy or Spain.

Chestnut soup is a treat any time, but the glorious feast of the Theophany as a conclusion to our Christmas celebrations gives us a unique occasion to enjoy this superb, rich soup—a true delight to our palates.

When the waters saw you, O God, when the waters saw you, they were afraid; the very deep trembled.

PSALM 77:16

CHESTNUT SOUP

6–8 SERVINGS

1 pound chestnuts in the shell
3 leeks, white and tender
    green parts only, thinly sliced
6 tablespoons butter or
    virgin olive oil
1 cup dry white wine
1 small acorn squash, peeled,
    hollowed out, and cut in
    small chunks
5 cups water
½ cup whole milk
Salt and freshly ground pepper

1 Preheat oven to 400° F.

2 Using a sharp knife, make an incision on the flat side of each chestnut. Lay chestnuts in a single layer on an ungreased baking sheet. Roast them for 15 to 20 minutes or until they turn fragrant. Remove sheet from oven and allow chestnuts to cool, then shell them and set apart the nutmeats.

3 Place leeks in a good-size soup pot and add 3 tablespoons of butter. Cook over low-medium heat, stirring continuously until leeks begin to sweat. Add wine and let it simmer for about 3 minutes. Add squash, all but ⅓ cup chestnuts, and water. Quickly bring mixture to a boil, then lower heat to low-medium and allow soup to simmer covered for another 20 to 25 minutes. Pour in milk and stir well. Allow to cool a bit.

4 Purée soup in batches in a blender until smooth. Pour soup back into pot and simmer over low heat. Season with salt and pepper to taste. If soup is too thick, thin with water or milk.

5 While soup simmers, melt remaining butter into a heavy skillet and sauté the remaining ⅓ cup of chestnuts. Add a dash of salt and pepper to taste, and stir continuously until chestnuts turn crisp and browned. Let stand. Serve soup in hot plates topped with crumbled chestnuts.

WE WHO LIVE in a freezing-weather zone face the grim and harsh reality of winter in several ways. In a monastery, one can do more reading and prayer as well as indoor creative work such as writing. One may also spend extra time in the kitchen by a warm stove, simmering a nourishing soup or baking hearty breads and tarts. I try to do a bit of all these, sometimes while observing our cherished monastic silence and other times while listening to an inspiring Bach cello suite or Beethoven quartet, which in my view don't interfere with the silence. To the contrary, good music seems to enhance the silence.

Unpredictable weather, short days, and long, dark, frigid nights can have a deep effect on the psyche. Creativity—reading, writing, playing, walking, working on craft projects, or cooking—is key to dealing constructively with our somber winter days as it uplifts our spirits and renews our souls. Creativity can also enhance our relationship with God in prayer and with the people whose lives surround us.

Today the monastic calendar keeps the memory of Saint Antony, the father of monks and my patron saint. I've always loved Saint Antony, and his example of Christian monastic living never ceases to inspire my pilgrimage. He's truly a humble servant of Christ, whom he preferred above all, a wise desert father whose inner radiance continues to shine. From the inhospitable Egyptian desert of the third and fourth centuries, he taught monks to seek God alone, to center our entire monastic lives on God. This he practiced daily through continual prayer, meditation on the Word of God, manual labor, discipline, charity toward his neighbors, silence, and continual recollection of God. Through the example of his life, he imparted wisdom to his disciples and encouraged them to remain

Do not fear then,

my children,

let Christ be

your life's breath,

and place all

your trust in Him.

Live as if dying daily.

SAINT ATHANASIUS
LIFE OF SAINT ANTONY:
HIS LAST COUNSELS

faithful to their monastic calling. I'm very grateful to Saint Antony for many things, particularly for his strong yet gentle presence here in our own little desert. This is very comforting to me.

Since Saint Antony was a very frugal monk, what better way to honor him at the table tonight than with a frugal meal? I think he would be pleased with that. There is plenty of leftover soup from last night to reheat today and serve as it was yesterday, followed by a salad of fresh greens, a morsel of cheese, and wholesome bread.

During the winter more than any other time of year, we need to see and taste those salad greens, a promise of the forthcoming spring. Eating fresh salads throughout our long winters is a good remedy for the psyche.

Our only treat tonight is a simple fruit compote—a dessert that warms us in more ways than one. Warm compotes always seem so nurturing during the cold season.

SAINT ANTONY WARM FRUIT COMPOTE

6–8 SERVINGS

1 vanilla bean, halved lengthwise
½ cup sugar (add more if necessary; follow your taste)
2 cups water
2 cups small dried apricots, whole
1 pound firm pears, peeled, seeded, and halved
2 tablespoons pear liqueur

OPTIONAL: 8 TEASPOONS CRÈME FRAÎCHE OR HEAVY CREAM

1 Cut vanilla bean lengthwise with a paring knife and scrape out seeds. Place bean, sugar, and water in a good-size pot. Stir and bring to a boil over medium heat.

2 Add apricots, pears, and liqueur. Cover and simmer slowly about 15 minutes. Stir from time to time. When fruits are cooked, turn off heat and cover again.

3 Check taste and add more sugar if needed. Keep compote hot to warm. Remove vanilla bean. Serve compote warm, reheating before serving if needed. As an option, top each serving with 1 teaspoon crème fraîche or heavy cream.

T HAS SNOWED nonstop anew, a blustering storm that paralyzed our area for three days. The heavy snow, the blasting wind, and the freezing temperature all made me eager for one of those hot, comforting, winter soups. Why is it that on days like these one instinctively turns to thoughts of soup? On a bitterly cold day such as today, we could relinquish all sorts of other pleasures at the table, but not that of a comforting and heart-warming soup. On a cold winter night, a roaring fire, a glass of red wine, and a bowl or two of a delicious hot soup is all that's needed to sufficiently nurture and satisfy us.

A good soup goes a long way to nourish not only our bodies, but also our souls. As I feed the corner wood stove in the kitchen and move around seeking more logs, I think about what kind of soup should feed the monastic table tonight. Something simple, light, and quick, with lots of comforting flavors and texture we could enjoy at supper right after our singing of Vespers.

Monks, professing a frugal way of life, never discard leftovers and always make a point of starting with them in planning the day's menu, so I start by searching for leftovers. Most of what I find this afternoon are fresh and frozen greens and some leeks in our cellar, so I decided to prepare a traditional green soup. Green soups are full of vitamins and minerals, and they're always delicious.

Beautiful soup,
so rich and green,
Waiting in a
hot tureen!
Who for such
dainties would
not stoop?
Soup of the evening,
beautiful soup!

LEWIS CARROLL

The main ingredients will be leeks harvested in November from our own garden and kept in our cellar, fresh escarole, and frozen Swiss chard and potatoes—these last two were also from our garden. I'll add minced garlic cloves to bring an aromatic touch to the soup.

The beauty and practicality of a good soup is that one can make it in sufficiently large portions to last two or three meals. In a monastery, just as in an ordinary home, monks don't mind repeating the same menu for several days as long as it hits the spot.

A GREEN SOUP
6–8 SERVINGS

10 tablespoons olive oil
6 garlic cloves, minced
    (more if you wish)
3 leeks, including the tender green
    parts, finely sliced
1 pound escarole greens,
    coarsely chopped
1 pound Swiss chard greens,
    top part only (or spinach or
    kale if you prefer), coarsely
    chopped
3 quarts water
2 bouillon cubes (vegetarian or
    other if you prefer)
4 medium-size potatoes, peeled
    and diced
Salt and freshly ground pepper
Grated Parmesan cheese

1 Pour oil into a good-size pot, add garlic and leeks, and sauté over low-medium heat for about 3 minutes, stirring often. Add escarole and Swiss chard greens. Continue to stir for another 2 to 3 minutes.

2 Add water, bouillon cubes, and potatoes, cover pot, and bring the soup to a quick boil. Lower heat to medium and allow soup to cook for 25 to 30 minutes. Add salt and pepper and more water if necessary. Lower heat to low-medium and simmer soup, covered, for another 10 minutes. Stir occasionally.

3 When soup is done, turn off heat and allow it to sit, covered, for about 5 minutes before serving. Serve soup hot and sprinkle grated cheese over each portion.

4 Reheat leftovers the following day, when the soup should taste even better.

RECENTLY I WAS ASKED to do a cooking demonstration for a church group in Westchester, New York. We had to plan and create a complete meal, so the first part of the menu consisted of a hot soup very appropriate for a cold January night. One of the participants asked whether, after a while, some soups don't become repetitive, especially those whose preparations require similar ingredients such as greens. My immediate response was that we can make soups often, at times using some of the similar ingredients, without having to repeat ourselves.

Take green soup. The greens can be used in a variety of ways, and the types of greens are endless: sorrel, chards, spinach, kale, cabbage, escarole, watercress, beet greens, turnip greens, broccoli rabe, and parsley. Depending on the green you choose, the flavor and the texture of each soup is distinct, earthy—even a bit mysterious. Add to all that the combination with vegetables, grains, or beans divergent from the ones used previously, and you end up with an entirely different soup.

Soup-making can be startling at times, as it can also be perplexing. Once you learn the formula for a good soup, you can recreate it again and again. You can also depart a bit from the recipe and create small variations from the original, and almost instantaneously you end up with a new recipe, a new soup. Throughout years of making and creating new soups, I have found that the secret asset of a good soup is its capacity, time and again, to reinvent itself.

See the miraculous in the ordinary, in the commonplace.

HENRY DAVID THOREAU

As an avid supporter of green soups in general and a strong believer in their nutritional aspects, I decide that tonight I'll prepare another green soup, a departure from the one we've consumed here the last couple of days. I'll use other varieties of greens and add acorn squash, tons of parsley, and navy beans instead of potatoes. I'll replace the leeks with onions. To make it even more different from the earlier green soup, this one can be puréed or blended, but that decision I leave for the last minute. I happen to like it both ways; blending the soup often extracts additional pungent and savory flavors from the greens, something not always readily achieved in a soup. I also enjoy the texture and flavor of the whole beans combined with the subtlety of the greens. This is such a good soup, it can be enjoyed both ways. *A la soupe!*

FRESH GREENS AND BEAN SOUP

6–8 SERVINGS

8 tablespoons olive oil
1 large Vidalia onion, coarsely chopped
6 garlic cloves, minced
3 quarts water
2 bouillon cubes (flavor of your preference)
1 acorn squash, peeled and cut in small chunks
2 cups precooked white navy beans
    or 2 cans of the same beans
1½ pounds fresh spinach, washed and
    coarsely chopped
10 sprigs Italian leafy parsley, chopped
2 teaspoons lemon juice
Salt and freshly ground pepper
Grated Parmesan cheese

1 Pour olive oil into a large soup pot. Add onion and sauté for 2 to 3 minutes over low-medium heat. Stir continuously. Add garlic and stir for another minute. Add water, bouillon cubes, squash, and beans. Cover pot, bring soup to a boil, and then reduce heat to low-medium. Cook for about 20 minutes.

2 Add spinach, parsley, and lemon juice. Cover pot and continue cooking over low-medium heat for another 20 minutes. Add salt and pepper. Simmer soup, covered, for about 10 minutes. Ladle soup into soup plates or bowls, and sprinkle grated Parmesan cheese on top as garnish. Serve hot.

Blending the soup and the addition of cream makes this recipe even more different from the earlier ones. Blending often extracts additional pungent and savory flavors from the greens, something not always readily achieved in a soup.

CREAM OF FRESH GREENS SOUP

6 SERVINGS

6 tablespoons olive oil
1 onion, chopped
1 head lettuce or escarole, finely chopped
1 bunch watercress, finely chopped
1 pound spinach, chopped
6 quarts water (more if necessary)
2 bouillon cubes
2 potatoes, sliced
1 pint heavy cream
Salt, nutmeg, and white pepper
Paprika

1 Pour the olive oil into the soup pot and sauté the onion slightly. Add the chopped greens, potatoes, bouillon cubes, and water. Boil the soup for 15 minutes and then simmer for another 15 minutes.

2 Blend the soup in a blender and return it to the pot. Add the heavy cream and seasonings and stir well. Reheat the soup and serve hot, sprinkling paprika on top of each serving.

FEBRUARY

*P*ART OF LIVING RIGHTLY in a monastery is to remain constantly in tune with the changing and flowing of the seasons, the months, the weeks, the days, the hours, and daybreak and nighttime. As our January days waned this past week, with one hand we said our goodbyes to the month till next year, quietly and without much fanfare. With the other, however, we began anticipating the next cycle and looking forward to brighter days.

Usually as January ends, here and there we begin to see signs of spring. One of the earliest signs, obviously, is the notable extension of the daylight. Slowly but surely, the winter darkness begins to recede, making room for extra daylight. Here in our rural monastery, one more sign is that our chickens begin laying eggs again after a few months of rest. Often, though not every year, as we reach the end of January just prior to Candlemas Day, the first egg suddenly appears in a nest in the barn where our chickens spend the winter with the sheep. The first few days I find an occasional egg, but as time progresses two or more eggs begin to show daily in some obscure corner of the barn. These small signs in a small farm monastery convey a certain truth: Half the winter season is over, no matter how many inches of snow may still be on the ground. The small seasonal signs point toward an exit from wintry days and make us anxious for what is to come.

Today is Candlemas, the feast of the Presentation of the Lord in the Temple. It's celebrated on the fortieth day after Christmas, and it's a fitting conclusion to the Christmas cycle. This deeply touching feast commemorates Mary and Joseph's carrying their infant son to the Temple to be presented to the Lord. At the Temple, the elder Simeon and the prophetess Anna anxiously await the appearance of the infant,

bursting into inexpressible joy when they see him. Looking back on the event, we realize Simeon and Anna had waited all these long years for this very day. They know him to be the Savior, the Promised One of Israel. As they meet the helpless infant and receive him for the first time in their arms, their tender joy cannot be contained. Filled with gratitude, they give thanks and praise to the Lord.

Candles have a central place in this day's liturgical celebration. The candles are blessed at the beginning of the liturgy as we prepare to enter the church in procession. This liturgical gesture reminds me that candles play a unique role in the devotional life of those following the monastic path. In a monastery, the candles of the Advent wreath and the Christmas candle symbolize Christ's presence in our midst, and the Easter candle is lit throughout paschaltime. Everyday candles are used during the celebration of the Eucharist and the monastic Offices, and the candles and oil lamps that burn in front of our icons symbolize our prayers and supplications. Candles are at our dinner tables, and candles accompany the Eucharist taken to a sick or dying monk in his cell.

The quiet yet steady flames of those candles in their proper setting speak volumes to the monastic heart. In their own way they offer comfort and solace in times of need; they also express our worship and adoration to the eternal God. Those simple wax candles, made by human hands yet imparting a mystical quality and grace, portray the presence of he who is the Light of the world. They serve as silent witnesses to the intangible realities of the world to come.

Because today is a special feast in the life of the monastery, some extra preparations must be made in the kitchen for the evening festive meal. "As the feast, so is the meal," an old monk assigned to the kitchen for well over 50 years used to repeat.

Two principles must be considered in today's meal: the cold weather and the moderation demanded of a monastic diet. Monks observe a monastic fast from September 14 until Easter, except for Sundays and feast days. It is amazing, however, how much one can create within the confines of these monastic principles.

The main menu for tonight consists of an oven-baked thick polenta accompanied by a tian of zucchini, eggplants, and onions. This will be followed by a plain endive salad and a small dessert. Polenta is as versatile as rice or pasta, can be prepared quickly, and is also most welcome on a cold February night. A tian of vegetables has all the advantages of grilling, extracting from the vegetables all their sweetness and flavors, and is quick and simple to prepare.

It would have been nice to add tomatoes to the tian as they often do in Provence, but I'm afraid we may have to wait until the summer months for that. Tonight, as we consume our evening meal, the large Christ candle will shine on us all from the center of the table. It's a candle that accompanies us during our meals on feast days and special occasions. The radiant light from the Christ candle never ceases to convey warmth, cheer, and a gentle glow. The presence of the candle is also a reminder of Christ's presence in our midst. He is here, with us at the table, to comfort us.

Endless variations exist for preparing polenta, but tonight's recipe is a thick one that involves the combination of winter squash, which are readily available at this time, and sautéed onion. To move quickly with the process, I first cook the squash separately, mash it, and then add it to the polenta. The same applies to the onion.

THICK MONASTIC POLENTA

6–8 SERVINGS

1 butternut squash, peeled, seeded, and cut in chunks
1 acorn squash, peeled, seeded, and cut in chunks
Olive oil
1 large onion, peeled and sliced
2 tablespoons fresh or dried minced sage (or rosemary)
6 cups water
Sea salt
1 cup coarse polenta
Freshly ground pepper
⅓ cup Parmigiano-Reggiano grated cheese or other of your preference
Butter
1 egg
2 tablespoons milk

1 Prepare butternut and acorn squash as indicated. Boil them in salted water until cooked. Drain thoroughly and then mash until even and creamy. Set aside.

2 Pour olive oil into a large skillet and sauté onion 2 to 3 minutes over low-medium heat. Add sage and stir continuously. Set aside.

3 Bring water to a boil in a good-size saucepan and add two or three teaspoons of olive oil and sea salt to taste. When liquid is boiling, slowly stir in polenta, stirring continuously until the mixture thickens. In 3 to 4 minutes, when polenta is cooked, turn off heat and slowly add cooked squash, onion, pepper, and cheese. Stir well until evenly mixed.

4 Thoroughly butter an elongated baking dish. Spoon polenta into the dish evenly until it reaches the top. Smooth with a spatula. Beat 1 egg and 2 tablespoons of milk and spread evenly over polenta with a kitchen brush. Bake at 350° F for 30 to 40 minutes until polenta is done. Serve hot accompanied by the tian of vegetables. A happy and blessed Candlemas Day to all!

TIAN OF VEGETABLES

6–8 SERVINGS

4 medium-size zucchini, washed and evenly sliced in circles
5 Japanese eggplant, washed and evenly sliced in circles
1 medium-size onion, chopped
2 garlic cloves, minced
1 teaspoon dried thyme leaves (or oregano)
6 tablespoons extra-virgin olive oil
3 tablespoons balsamic vinegar
Salt and freshly ground pepper
Butter

1 Place vegetables, onion, garlic, and thyme in a deep bowl. Pour in oil and vinegar and add salt and pepper.
Stir gently until vegetables are well coated.
Marinate for 1 or 2 hours.

2 Thoroughly butter an elongated baking dish and arrange vegetables next to each other in row order: row 1, zucchini; row 2, eggplant; and so forth. Pour juice from the marinade sauce and its contents evenly over the top of the vegetables. Cover baking dish with foil and bake at 350° F for 25 to 30 minutes. Serve hot as an accompaniment to the polenta.

TREASURE the quiet moments in our monastery kitchen. Exterior and interior silence are a must in the monastic life, including the hours spent working in the kitchen. Our lifestyle demands a certain quiet that makes every moment propitious for prayer, for listening, for compassion, for understanding. It's not unusual, therefore, that a silent atmosphere permeates an otherwise busy and bustling kitchen. Silence enhances the precious hours spent there as it enhances the work itself; silence always makes for better concentration, which is integral to good cooking.

For monks, silence is a form of respect for the presence of God and for each other. We know the Lord is present with us at all times, but we need a certain quiet and silence to remind ourselves of that. Silence also makes us ready for a quiet rapport with God as we busily labor with our hands. Silence enhances the quality of that conversation.

Silence and music invariably go together. While silently peeling vegetables, making a soup, or preparing a dessert, we occasionally listen to fine music, which in my view, never alters or disturbs the monastic silence. On the contrary, serious music such as that of Bach, Beethoven, Haydn, Mozart, Schumann, or Brahms allows us to discover inner harmony within the confines of a silent monastic life. Such music, containing both aspects of the human and the divine, never ceases to nurture the human spirit and leads us ultimately to the ineffable mystery of God. They make my work in the kitchen a thousand times more agreeable while enriching the long stretches of our winter days with an incontestably profound experience.

Because of my many extra monastic chores, which I must say pragmatically include working on this book, I've planned a simple and uncomplicated soup that will save me a bit of cooking time to give me

In the silence of the heart, tirelessly God whispers to each of us, "Don't be afraid. I am here." Wait for God, even when body and spirit are dry and parched.

BROTHER ROGER OF TAIZÉ

more writing time. This soup, which consists of mushrooms, barley, some winter vegetables, and plenty of garlic, can be prepared well in advance and reheated at the last minute. It's fitting for a blustery cold day like today, with the snow falling and the wind blowing in all four directions. After all, what a good and comforting feeling we'll receive from a hot, nurturing soup on a freezing night! *N'est-ce pas?* Nothing can replace that feeling!

MUSHROOM-BARLEY-SQUASH AND GARLIC SOUP
6–8 SERVINGS

½ cup dried porcini mushrooms
8 tablespoons olive oil
1 large Vidalia onion (or other),
    chopped
8 garlic cloves, minced
3 celery stalks, thinly sliced
½ pound white mushrooms,
    washed and coarsely chopped
2 medium-size carrots, diced
3 quarts water (more if needed)
1 acorn squash, peeled, seeded,
    and cut into small chunks
½ cup barley, rinsed
1 bay leaf
½ cup dry white wine
2 teaspoons cornstarch or flour
Sea salt and freshly ground pepper
Small bunch fresh parsley,
    finely chopped

1 Soak dried mushrooms in water for about 1 hour. Drain them. Coarsely chop and set them aside.

2 Pour oil into a large soup pot and heat it over a low-medium flame. Add onion, garlic, celery, mushrooms, and carrots. Sauté for 7 to 8 minutes until vegetables turn soft. Stir often.

3 Add water and raise heat to medium-high. Bring soup to a quick boil, cover pot and cook for about 15 minutes. Add squash, barley, and bay leaf. Lower heat to medium, cover pot, and continue cooking for another 30 minutes. Add more water if needed.

4 In ½ cup white wine, stir and dissolve cornstarch or flour. Pour mixture into soup, add salt, pepper, and chopped parsley. Stir the soup, cover pot, and continue cooking over low-medium heat for 10 to 15 minutes. Adjust the soup, adding a tiny bit more water if necessary and checking the seasonings. Just before serving, remove the bay leaf. Serve the soup hot.

ESTERDAY was one of those winter days one doesn't easily forget. We had a roaring storm, with wild gusts of northern winds directing the snowfall across the entire countryside. The roads were closed, the snowdrifts high above the farm fences, and the monastery roof covered with inches and inches of snow. Another northeaster. A blizzard is not unusual at this time of the year, but we're never really prepared for it. We continue to hope we'll escape these storms, but it's too much to hope for.

I struggle to reach the barn to feed the sheep, in some ways delighting in the blanket of snow that surrounds the countryside, so white and so still. The air is so sharp, so frosty—almost exhilarating.

When I return to the monastery, I sit for a moment in front of the open fire to warm myself and reflect. God made the world so all his creatures are inextricably linked. The welfare of each is the welfare of all. That's the ideal Jesus preached, lived, and died for. This is enough reason to persevere in a monastery until death, enough reason to continue writing and sharing the Good News with those of goodwill.

The snow is quite heavy. This is not totally unusual on the feast of Saint Scholastica. But in spite of the weather, today's feast is cause for joy. After all, Saint Scholastica is the twin sister of our father Saint Benedict, and she herself is considered the mother of nuns.

Saint Scholastica was very subdued and serene and lived in the shadow of her famous brother. A woman of deep faith, she was totally involved in the work of prayer. She was also a woman of deep sensibilities and exquisite charm. She brought these qualities into the cloister when she embraced the monastic life. She followed the tradition of the early women monastics in the desert in that she not only tried to mimic the virtues and fervor of monks—she often actually surpassed them.

The feast of Saint Scholastica, for us monks, is an intimate family feast, and today's menu will reflect this. I often think how unfortunate it is that many families have lost the practice of eating together. Life in a monastery tends to be just the opposite. I'm deeply grateful that both *The Rule of Saint Benedict* and our ancient tradition exhort the monks not only to pray together, but to work and eat together as well. The sacrament of the table, like the sacrament of the Eucharist, is meant to be shared. In a sense, both become the visible symbol of unity of the monastic family.

To enhance our intimate family feast today, I've decided to prepare a soup of roasted butternut squash as a first course. Served in warm plates or bowls, soup offers comfort and solace on cold days. In this recipe, the squash is roasted beforehand. This method takes a bit longer, but small details such as these make the difference between the simple soup of an ordinary day and the more complex one of a festive meal. In the life of a monastery, those subtle differences mean a lot.

This soup may be prepared ahead of time and then refrigerated, although I prefer to make it the day it's consumed. Adding a little cream to the soup contributes a special French touch, and the nutmeg and herbs from Provence enhance the soup's appeal enormously.

ROASTED BUTTERNUT SQUASH SOUP

6–8 SERVINGS

3 butternut squash
Butter
Olive oil
Honey or maple syrup,
    as needed
4 medium leeks,
    washed and thinly
    sliced in circles,
    including the
    tender greens
2 medium-size carrots,
    peeled and diced
10 cups water or
    vegetable broth
½ teaspoon nutmeg
Sea salt and freshly
    ground pepper
2 teaspoons dried thyme,
    sage, and rosemary
    from Provence
½ cup heavy cream

1 Halve squash lengthwise and scrape out the seeds. Rub butter over the surface. Place 1 teaspoon of honey or maple syrup in each cavity, and roast at 375° F on the lower rack of the oven for about 30 minutes or until they turn soft. Remove the halves from the oven. Allow them to cool, and then scoop out the squash and lay aside. Discard the peels.

2 Pour 6 tablespoons of olive oil into a soup pot and add leeks and carrots. Sauté over medium heat, stirring often, for 4 to 5 minutes. Add the roasted squash, water or broth, nutmeg, salt and pepper, and herbs from Provence. Raise heat to medium-high and bring soup to a boil. Reduce heat to low-medium, cover pot, and simmer soup slowly for about 30 minutes. Add more water if needed. After soup is done, turn off heat and allow it to cool.

3 Strain vegetables with a large colander and save the liquid. Mash vegetables or purée them in a blender. Add cream to the blender and purée mixture until smooth.

4 Return vegetable mixture to the soup pot, add liquid kept aside and more water if needed. Reheat soup at low-medium and stir often. Taste and check seasonings. Adjust them. Add more water if soup is too thick, or substitute low-fat milk for water. Serve soup hot. As garnish, add 1 teaspoon of cream at the center of each serving.

Our main course will be a three-cheese omelette. Omelettes are quick to make and always appetizing. In monasteries, omelettes are usually part of the main meal and not a breakfast staple as is the custom in the United States. I can't think of another culinary endeavor as dependable and satisfying as a well-prepared omelette. There is something enchanting about combining eggs, Gruyère, a goat cheese, a Stilton, or any other cheese and then applying instant heat to them.

The result is pure magic!

OMELETTE AU TROIS FROMAGES
(Three-Cheese Omelet)

4–6 SERVINGS

2 tablespoons unsalted butter

8 eggs, lightly beaten

4 teaspoons milk

Salt and freshly ground pepper

½ cup grated Gruyère cheese

⅓ cup Stilton cheese, crumbled

⅓ cup goat cheese, crumbled

⅓ cup fresh chives,
    finely chopped

1 Heat well a large cast-iron omelette pan. Melt the butter over high heat. When bubbles begin to die down, add egg mixture and let it run over the entire surface of the pan. Evenly distribute cheeses over the egg surface. Do the same with the chives, making sure every corner of the omelette is covered. Cover pan with a large lid for 1 or 2 minutes to help melt cheeses. Tip the pan back and forth a few times and lift the omelette edges with the help of a large spatula. Let the liquid from the eggs run underneath.

2 The moment the surface of the omelette is no longer runny but is still creamy and loose, fold it in three lengthwise segments by simply flipping the edges towards the center. When the omelette is done, cut it in 4 or 6 slices and gently slide each piece into a hot plate. Serve hot.

To accompany this rich omelette, I'll add a side dish of plain haricot verts. We still have quite an amount in our freezer, the result of a good monastic harvest, and we must use them before the next season. A touch of lemon will make the beans almost sublime.

LEMONY GREEN BEANS

2 pounds small fine string beans
   (*haricots verts*), washed and
   trimmed (frozen is fine)
4 tablespoons extra-virgin olive oil
Salt and freshly ground pepper
⅔ teaspoon finely grated fresh
   lemon zest (or 1 teaspoon
   fresh lemon juice)

1 Fill a large saucepan with water, add salt, and bring to a boil. Lower heat to medium–high, add beans and cook 5 to 6 minutes until tender. Just before serving, drain the beans.

2 Place beans in a deep bowl, add olive oil, freshly ground pepper (more salt if needed), and lemon zest (or lemon juice). Toss gently and serve as side accompaniment to the omelette.

SAINT SCHOLASTICA BREAD PUDDING

Butter
3 large, fresh eggs
3 cups milk
½ cup sugar
Pinch of cinnamon
Pinch of nutmeg
¼ cup brandy or rum
10 slices of good-quality brown
   bread, cut in triangles
6 apples, peeled, cored,
   and cut into thin slices
½ cup raisins

OPTIONAL:
6 TABLESPOONS MAPLE SYRUP;
6 TABLESPOONS HEAVY CREAM

1 Thoroughly butter an elongated, ovenproof dish (7 inches by 9 inches by 2 inches). Preheat oven to 350° F.

2 Place eggs, milk, sugar, cinnamon, nutmeg, and brandy in a blender. Whirl ingredients for 2 to 3 minutes, until it is evenly blended. Set aside.

3 Pour small amount of egg-milk mixture over the surface of the dish and let it run over entire surface. Arrange bread pieces to cover entire surface. Add apple slices on top. Evenly distribute half of the raisins over apples. Pour a small amount of egg-milk mixture over the entire top. Repeat process once more: 1 layer of bread pieces, 1 layer of apple slices, and 1 layer of raisins. Pour the rest of the egg-milk mixture over entire surface, making sure every inch of the surface is covered. Let stand for at least 5 minutes. If desired, distribute maple syrup over the top more or less evenly. Use a spatula if needed. Bake pudding about 30 minutes until done. Remove from oven and let stand about 10 minutes before serving.

4 Slice into 6 or 8 pieces, pour heavy cream over the top (optional), and serve warm.

HERE ISN'T A DOUBT in my mind about the value of tradition in real life. Every monastery—indeed every country, locality, or family—relies on the living memory and treasures from their past to make sense of their present. Tradition is that mysterious unbroken line that emerges from the past, allowing us to feel connected to something larger than ourselves.

This is as true in the kitchen as in any other aspect of life. It isn't surprising, for example, that we repeat the same dishes (with some variations, of course) on yearly celebrations like Thanksgiving, Christmas, Easter, Fourth of July, Valentine's Day. It's not surprising to hear on Thanksgiving Day that the recipe for the pumpkin pie comes from Grandma or that the rolls and muffins were made according to Aunt Margaret's recipe.

Yet, for tradition to survive, it must relate to the here and now. It can't simply rot in the memory of an idealized past—it must constantly reinvent itself. Tradition must make sense to everyone; it must continue to find its voice and *raison d'etre* in the present.

In the monastery, an example of our adherence to culinary traditions is our consumption of soups, often twice a day. For centuries the European monasteries have served soups as an everyday staple. Today, to continue serving soups 365 days of the year, one needs to be a bit imaginative to improve their quality and appeal. A couple of years ago, I realized that for the tradition of soups to survive in the monastic diet, it had to be adapted, renewed, and experimented with. I needed to try new concepts, new recipes, new ideas. This was the origin of *Twelve Months of Monastery Soups*, a book that has been translated into several languages and has sold over 350,000 copies.

Tonight's soup isn't extraordinary; however, small touches here and there make

*A long year
must pass
before the truths
we have made
for ourselves
become
our very flesh.*

PAUL VALERY

it special. I begin by replacing the traditional onions with the more subtle leeks. Leeks furnish a smoother, more discriminating taste to the soup, and they happen to blend well with the asparagus. But what really gives this soup its unique, genteel flavor is the lemon zest. When I prepare this soup for guests, people suddenly ask, what is that special spice? They don't always recognize it instantly. A few touches like that, plus the creamy character of the soup, make it a new version of an older recipe. Tradition and innovation blend perfectly in this case.

CREAM OF LEEK AND ASPARAGUS SOUP
6–8 SERVINGS

6 tablespoons olive oil
3 leeks, washed and thinly sliced,
 including parts of their tender greens
2 medium-size potatoes, peeled and cubed
7 cups water or vegetable stock
 (or chicken stock for nonvegetarians)
1½ teaspoons grated lemon zest
1 pound fresh asparagus,
 trimmed and cut into small pieces
½ cup half-and-half (more if needed or desired)
Sea salt and white pepper

OPTIONAL: FRESHLY CHOPPED PARSLEY

1 Pour olive oil into a large soup pot. Add leeks and potatoes and sauté over low-medium heat for 4 to 5 minutes or until soft. Stir often.

2 Add water or stock, lemon zest and asparagus. Cover pot and cook for 25 to 30 minutes. Add more water if needed. Allow soup to cool.

3 Purée soup in a blender and return it to the pot. Add half-and-half and seasonings to taste. Reheat soup for a few minutes until hot (no need to reboil). When ready to serve, remove from heat, stir once more, and serve hot. Add freshly chopped parsley to the top as garnish (optional).

AS I SIT DOWN to write on this wintry morning, I'm reminded that in France today is the memorial feast of Saint Bernadette, a humble shepherdess from the Pyrenees. She's very dear to me for many reasons, one being that we both issue from the same sturdy Pyrenees mountain people. Those mountains we love so dearly are in our blood. Little Bernadette was very attached to them as she tended her flock of sheep. It was in the silence of those majestic mountains that she opened herself to God, to his special designs for her. The rugged life in her beloved mountains was God's means of preparing her for the events that would change her simple life.

On February 11, 1858, the Blessed Mother of God appeared to Bernadette in the grotto of Massabielle, a niche carved into the mountains. The apparitions continued for months, during which time Our Lady confided to the little shepherdess many secrets. I don't doubt that this humble peasant from the Pyrenees was chosen to witness these heavenly visitations because of her deep humility. She never, before or after the apparitions, attributed anything good to herself, only to God. Her profound humility is a constant inspiration to we who love the simple shepherdess.

Nothing is so welcoming on a winter night as a bowl of hot soup. On cold days like today, I often have two bowls of hot soup and two slices of bread as my evening meal. I feel nourished, comforted, and warm, both in body and spirit.

The basic simplicity of soup gives it a timeless appeal. When I was growing up, the "souper" always consisted of a good homemade soup and plenty of it. My family, descendants of the mountain people of the Pyrenees, were proud of their heritage. My grandmother often prepared a local soup called *garbure*. We often feasted on it during long, cold winter nights.

Soups were the usual daily fare of monasteries throughout the centuries. They are also the daily fare of the poor and the homeless who seek relief in soup kitchens like those sponsored by the Catholic Worker Movement founded by Dorothy Day.

I live by good soup, and not on fine language.

MOLIÈRE
THE LEARNED LADIES

Feast of
SAINT BERNADETTE

I was privileged to share many a bowl of soup with her both in Tivoli and in New York City. She said soup was never missing from a Catholic Worker table.

When I make a simple, basic soup for myself, I use whatever ingredients are available. Tonight I found an onion, a carrot, celery, and a potato and decided to make a plain pea soup. I sautéed the onion, then added a couple of cups of water, the diced carrot and potato, thinly sliced celery (three branches), and dried split peas. When the water began boiling, I added one bay leaf (rescued from a bay plant in the greenhouse, a plant we've grown here for over twenty-five years), a pinch of salt and pepper, a minced garlic clove, and some finely chopped fresh parsley. I allowed the soup to cook slowly over medium heat until it was ready.

For the feast of Saint Bernadette, we'll have that soup, followed by a small piece of Pyrenees cheese accompanied by bread and a plain green salad, just the way the people of the Pyrenees would have eaten. Tonight's dessert, however, will be something special. This famous dessert has endless variations, but our own unique secret is to prepare it with the freshest of ingredients and much love, as our mountain ancestors have done throughout the centuries. *Bon appétit!*

SAINT BERNADETTE'S CREAMY RICE PUDDING   6–8 SERVINGS

10 cups milk
2 cinnamon sticks
1 teaspoon
    grated lemon zest
1 cup white rice,
    arborio or similar
1 cup sugar
2 tablespoons
    Armagnac liqueur
Ground cinnamon

1 Pour milk into a good-size saucepan and bring it to a quick boil. Add cinnamon sticks and lemon zest and continue boiling over medium-high heat for 5 to 6 minutes. Reduce heat to low, add rice, cover saucepan, and allow rice to cook for 1 ½ hours or until it turns into a creamy mixture. Stir often to keep the rice from sticking to the bottom of the saucepan.

2 When rice is cooked, remove and discard cinnamon sticks and lemon zest. Slowly and evenly pour sugar through a sieve into the rice pudding. Stir gently and continue to cook over low heat for 10 to 15 minutes or until the pudding is done.

3 Remove saucepan from heat and allow it to cool. Refrigerate it or serve it lukewarm, especially during the winter. Sprinkle ground cinnamon over the top as garnish. (One can also add 2 tablespoons of heavy cream on top of each serving for a creamier version.)

AS FEBRUARY reaches its end, one begins to see some changes. With all the February flip-flops we endure here in the Northeast, it's hard to let go of the theme of hot soups. They seem so appropriate for the season, and I don't mean just any soups. I refer more to those aromatic, all-day-simmered soups rich in herbs and spices whose fragrance pervades and perfumes the entire kitchen. Both children and adults enjoy such body- and mind-restoring soups.

Occasionally parents tell me their children don't like soup. I tell them to make the soups more aromatic, letting the fragrance seduce the noses and palates of their little ones. Furthermore, I also suggest they offer the children some rich *tartines*, slices of toast with melted cheese with the soup. It's a perfect trick to win over young appetites, for who can refuse a delicious piece of bread covered in sumptuous melted cheese? Children and adults easily fall for it.

The idea of a good soup accompanied often by a warm *tartine* is nothing new. It's not only done in many homes and monasteries in France, but also in some very chic restaurants. At a famous restaurant in Toulouse, *Ras le Bol,* the speciality of the house is soup served in the old-fashioned *soupieres* accompanied by a series of delicious, generously sized *tartines,* usually large slices of a good bread covered with cheese and placed briefly under the grill or in the oven. The tops can be covered with quality meat such as hams, mushrooms, vegetables, or a combination. These appetizing *tartines* complement the soup and complete the meal.

The gentle art of gastronomy is a friendly one. It hurdles the language barrier, makes friends among civilized people, and warms the heart.

SAMUEL CHAMBERLAIN

(1895–1975)

This sort of menu is popular in many households for, in the view of many parents, the *tartines* are an added incentive for the children to eat and enjoy a nutritious soup. On days when the cook doesn't wish to initiate an elaborate menu, a good soup escorted by appetizing *tartines* is the perfect solution.

The secret of a good *tartine* is to always serve it as it comes out of the oven. Tonight I'll offer two or three different types of tartines with the evening soup.

WINTER VEGETABLE SOUP WITH FINE HERBS
6–8 SERVINGS

8 tablespoons olive oil
1 large onion, coarsely chopped
2 leeks, thinly sliced, including
    parts of the bottom greens
3 medium carrots, peeled and diced
1 medium turnip, diced
2 celery stalks, finely sliced
12 cups water or vegetable stock
2 garlic cloves, minced
1 bay leaf
½ cup white rice
4 tablespoons fine herbs
    from Provence (thyme, rosemary,
    oregano, basil)
3 parsley sprigs, finely chopped
1 cup white dried wine
Salt and pepper
Grated Pecorino cheese

1 Pour olive oil into a large soup pot. Add onion, leeks, carrots, turnip, and celery; sauté lightly over low-medium heat for 3 to 4 minutes. Stir continuously.

2 Add water or stock, garlic, bay leaf, rice, Provence herbs, parsley and wine. Raise heat to medium-high, cover pot, and bring soup to a quick boil. After boiling 8 to 10 minutes, lower heat to low-medium, cover pot, and let it simmer for 25 to 30 minutes. Add salt and pepper to taste, cover pot, and simmer for 5 more minutes. Serve soup hot. Sprinkle grated Pecorino cheese on top as garnish. Serve with the tartines described next. You need an average of 2 tartines per person.

TARTINE DE LUBERON (Toast From the Luberon)

4–6 SERVINGS

1 large loaf of good-quality
  French bread, halved lengthwise
Several slices of Swiss cheese,
  or Jalsberg (or other) to
  cover both slices
5 tablespoons olive oil, or the
  equivalent in butter if preferred
1 medium onion, finely chopped
1 green bell pepper, finely chopped
⅓ cup chopped red pimentos
⅓ cup chopped fresh parsley
2 celery sticks, thinly sliced
Virgin olive oil

1 Cut each bread half into four equal parts so as to have 8 even slices. Place the slices in an ovenproof long pan. Cover bread with cheese slices and set aside.

2 Pour oil or butter into a frying pan, add remaining ingredients. Sauté lightly over low-medium heat for 3 to 5 minutes or until tender.
Stir almost constantly. Spread vegetables evenly over bread. Drizzle olive oil on top. Place pan in the oven at 300° F for 10 to 15 minutes or until cheese melts. Serve hot with soup.

TARTINE DE LOURMARIN (Toast From Lourmarin)

4 SERVINGS

4 good-quality English muffins,
  halved, or another type of bread
2 4-ounce packages of goat cheese
8 tablespoons extra-virgin olive oil
1 tablespoon cognac
3 tablespoons herbs from Provence
  (thyme, basil, oregano, rosemary,
  bay leaf), crumbled
8 pitted black olives, finely chopped
Salt and pepper

1 Arrange English muffin slices on an oven-proof pan and set aside. (If you wish, butter or oil the pan before arranging the slices.)

2 Cut goat cheese into small pieces and place them in a deep bowl. Crumble cheese with a fork. Add olive oil, cognac, dried herbs from Provence, chopped olives, salt, and pepper to taste.
(I almost never add salt, for the cheese contains salt.)
Mix ingredients thoroughly. Add more oil if needed. Spread cheese mixture evenly over muffin or bread slices. Place them in the oven at 300° F for 15 to 20 minutes. Serve hot, 2 slices per person, as accompaniment to the soup.

MARCH

ARCH is certainly a month of contrasts. We can have warm, springlike weather one day, and then the following day takes us back to winter with a sudden blizzard or heavy downpour. Today it's windy and raw, yet the first snowdrops are beginning to blossom around the stone statue of Our Lady. In the distance I can see a subtle tone of green slowly making its return to our fields and pastures. Spring is still quite a few weeks away, and I'm growing impatient for its arrival. The winter has been long and hard, and every year at this time I experience the same longing, the same desire, the same impatience for spring.

March is a forward-looking month—at least I see it that way. On my daily walks in the monastic enclosure, I can feel the stirrings of the land. The approaching spring seems to be rising in the horizon with the subtle rays of the sun, in the deep clean fresh country air we breathe, and ultimately in the depths of the human heart. Deep within, we long for spring's eternal promises, its sense of hope that seems to breathe new life into all of us.

The month of March almost always coincides with our Lenten pilgrimage. Every year, Lent returns in February or March. Lent is a very special time in a monastery, so much that Saint Benedict declared that the life of a monk must retain at all times a "Lenten character." Our Lenten pilgrimage is a time of intense preparation to welcome the Pasch of the Lord: Easter, the Feast of Feasts.

Since Lent is essentially a penitential season, there is a moderate amount of fasting in a monastery. Our monastic diet seeks ways of combining the frugality of Lent with healthy, nutritious dishes to sustain us throughout the journey. Fasting is a very interesting discipline. While it invites us to be frugal and moderate in our use of food and drink, it acknowledges the necessity of physical strength to sustain us. That strength can come only from a predetermined amount of food consumption.

During Lent we typically continue to consume soups every day, but often instead of a main course we prepare a variety of tartines to accompany the soup. That's a complete meal—these tartines always have bread and cheese as a base, for cheese provides the necessary protein in our daily diet.

*The stormy March
is come at last,
With wind,
and cloud, and
changing skies;
I hear the rushing
of the blast,
That through the
snowy valley flies.*

WILLIAM CULLEN BRYANT

CROUSTADES ESPAGNOLES (Spanish Toasts)

8 slices fresh country bread
(*pain de campagne*) or other
of your preference
⅓ cup white dry wine
12 ounces Manchego cheese
(made from sheep's milk);
if not available, use goat cheese
1 teaspoon dried oregano
4 garlic cloves, minced
4 tablespoons virgin olive oil
1 egg
Salt and freshly ground pepper

1 Place bread slices into an ovenproof tray and preheat the oven to 300° F.

2 Pour wine into a small casserole dish and heat over low flame. Crumble cheese and add it to the wine, dried oregano, minced garlic, and olive oil. Stir continuously until ingredients dissolve into a creamy consistency. Set aside.

3 In a deep bowl, beat the egg, add salt and pepper, and beat some more. Add the wine-cheese mixture and blend thoroughly with egg. Spread this mixture evenly on the bread slices. There should be enough mixture for 6 to 8 slices, depending on size. Place tray in preheated oven for 4 to 5 minutes or until cheese mixture on top melts. Serve hot as accompaniment to a soup or a good salad.

Another tartine that's easy to make and always pleasing to the palate combines leeks and mushrooms. I've seen it served as an appetizer at elegant brunches or dinners. In that case, it requires an especially good bread as a base combined with quality cheese such as Stilton. The recipe given here is much simpler, and you can choose English muffins or any whole grain bread as a base. It's better and easier to eat this tartine with a fork and knife rather than with the hands.

TARTINE SUPERSTAR

8 slices rich whole grain bread
(or English muffins or other
bread of preference)
8 slices of Gouda cheese (or other
cheese of preference)
3 tablespoons cooking oil
2 medium-size leeks, finely sliced,
including the tender part
of the greens
¼ pound white mushrooms,
washed and thinly sliced
2 teaspoons dry Spanish sherry wine
Dash of salt and white pepper
4 tablespoons heavy cream

1 Butter well an ovenproof tray and place bread on it. Place cheese slices on bread and set aside. Preheat oven to 300° F.

2 Pour oil into a good-size skillet, add leeks and mushrooms, and sauté over low-medium heat for about 3 minutes. Stir frequently. Add sherry, salt, and pepper. Continue stirring for 1 or 2 minutes. At the last moment, add cream and stir for 1 minute. Turn off heat.

3 Spread this mixture evenly over each tartine. Place the tartine in the preheated oven for 4 to 5 minutes or until cheese melts. Remove tartines from oven and serve hot. Tartines can be eaten alone or as accompaniment to a good soup or salad.

EACH YEAR, no matter when Easter falls, Lent coincides with March. In the northeast, March also brings the wet season, when rain melts the icy snow and makes our roads muddy and impassable.

March isn't always pleasant. Once during early March, I received visitors from Japan who were interested in my methods of cooking. Just before they departed, I asked what they most enjoyed during their stay. They said they were very impressed with the silence and the tranquility of the monastery kitchen, that it inspired concentration and creativity in the art of cooking. When I asked about their dislikes, they readily mentioned the constant March rains, which they found quite depressing.

After they left, I reflected on their assessments. Yes, it's true that silence and tranquility inspire the order and prayer that helps facilitate creativity in our daily food preparation. But both silence and tranquility must not be taken for granted as ready achievements in a monastic atmosphere. On the contrary, constant effort and vigilance are necessary to preserve a tranquil and placid spirit in our kitchen as in other workplaces throughout the monastery.

As for the March rains, we can do nothing about those. I see them as a challenge to learn spiritual lessons. First, one must face discomfort by cultivating a resilient attitude, something that goes very well with our Lenten observance. A resilient spirit is always ready to accept reality—without complaining too much—when it comes to us in everyday events. Later in March the magical beauty of spring will arrive, and the sun will again warm our shoulders as we clear the garden for planting. Just a little bit longer and the days of spring, delight, and easy joy will be here to stay.

During these Lenten days I pay particular attention to the quality of our monastic diet. Lent is here to teach us about self-control, especially over our sensual appetites. Traditional Lenten practice encourages fasting and abstinence from meat to achieve control over our senses. Nevertheless, I think we can also ascertain other means of achieving the same end. For example, couldn't we abstain from popular entertainment and other worldly distractions to concentrate more on God, our own spiritual needs, and the needs of our neighbors? Wouldn't this kind of fasting and abstaining be closer to the kind of fasting Jesus taught in the Gospels? Fasting and abstinence from certain foods, while helpful when included as part of our Lenten practice, are not the only ways to keep the true spirit of Lent.

Saint Benedict's wise principle of "moderation in all things" helps me confront the realities of fasting and abstinence. As part of our Lenten observance, this rule

When a man leaves on a journey, he must know where he is going. Thus with Lent. Above all, Lent is a spiritual journey and its destination is Easter, "the Feast of Feasts."

ALEXANDER SCHMEMANN

has undeniable ascetic value. But I wonder how it could be adjusted today without compromising their intrinsic worth.

When asked about Lenten fasting and abstinence, I speak more and more about frugality and simplicity. These two concepts are in tune with our times. Frugality doesn't deny the reality or quality of the food we need, but it makes us aware of the cost and the amount strictly and personally needed by each. It makes us aware that we need only so much to sustain us in our daily journey, and no more.

Eggs and cheese are part and parcel of our Lenten fare because they provide the protein necessary to sustain us on our Lenten journey. We don't eat them every day, just often enough to maintain our physical and mental equilibrium.

During Lent I continue to prepare basic soups that warm the body and mind, usually accompanied by cheese in some form, such as the tartines I suggested earlier. When pressed for time, I prepare cold tartines that needn't be put in the oven. Cold tartines are more appetizing during the summer than during the raw cold evenings of March, but this is Lent, so they can be considered part of our asceticism. No one has ever complained since, after all, a cold tartine does as much to cure hunger pangs as hot melting ones. The difference lies in the attraction we have for hot, melting cheese, especially on a chilly winter night.

TARTINES A LA MOZZARELLA (Mozzarella Toasts)

6 SERVINGS

**6 slices of fresh whole-wheat bread
(if not fresh, toast slightly before serving)**
Butter
6 slices of fresh mozzarella cheese
6 tomato slices
6 teaspoons extra-virgin olive oil
½ small red onion, finely chopped
6 pitted black olives, coarsely chopped
A few sprigs of fresh parsley, finely chopped

1 Butter 6 bread slices lightly.

2 Place a slice of mozzarella cheese slice on each slice of bread. Top each with a tomato slice.

3 Pour olive oil into a bowl, add chopped onion, black olives, and parsley. Mix well. Just before serving, spread mixture evenly over the tartines and serve immediately. (If you prefer them warm, place them in the oven for a few minutes or until cheese begins to melt.)

THE LONG WINTER SECLUSION seems to be receding, and part of me doesn't wish to let go. After all, quiet winter days and their calm evenings are great promoters of the craft of writing. I ventured outdoors early this morning to find the first open daffodils. This cluster is protected by their proximity to the monastery, and every year on that spot I see the first promise of spring.

As I gently gaze on those fresh first daffodils, I feel so thankful to God for placing me on this small corner of his world where I can see, smell, feel, hear, and be filled with wonder at the gifts of his creation. On days like today, it's good to feel alive, to say, "Yes, I am truly here. *Deo gratias!*" Wonder of wonders—yesterday's fierce, wild gusts of northern wind seem a distant memory. Today, Mother Nature seems so still and placid, revealing quietly in these first daffodils the exhilarating promises of the quickly approaching season.

It's cleaning day in the kitchen, a task I don't always relish, but today I'll consider it part of the asceticism demanded by the Lenten season. It's good penance to embrace from time to time a task we don't hold in high esteem.

After the task is completed, I'll enjoy having a neat, clean kitchen in which to work and smell the sweet, fresh aroma from both the cooking and the wood burning in a clean stove. A friend used to repeat to me, "A clean kitchen is a thing of beauty, a joy forever." I think he was right, for beauty in the kitchen is experienced at many levels, including the spiritual. As I get deeply involved in the small details of cleaning, I continue to reflect on the meaning of our Lenten journey. One of the good things about menial manual work is that it can be performed quietly, in silence, thus freeing the mind for reflection and prayer. As I meditate, I also begin to plan the menu for the main meal, mindful that on a Lenten weekday our menu must reflect the sobriety of the season.

Rice is one of our favorite staples during Lent, for it is quite versatile and can be reinvented in many ways. For instance, you can make a delicious soufflé or croquettes or the base for a soup with winter vegetables. Today's main course is a risotto that's topped with a fresh, lightly fried egg, thus making the risotto juicy and appetizing. It's an old Italian rustic recipe that has survived the passing of the centuries, mostly in monasteries of Italy, France, and Spain, and in many peasant homes from the same regions. In today's recipe, the rice will be accompanied by a simple plain green salad. The rice-and-egg combination is particularly practical during the Lenten period, for the eggs provide the protein needed to make the dish a complete meal.

*Daffodils
That come before
the swallow
dares, to take
The winds
of March
with beauty.*

SHAKESPEARE

PEA RISOTTO

4–6 SERVINGS

3 tablespoons butter or olive oil
1 medium-size white Vidalia onion
   (or other)
1 pound frozen peas
1 cup dry white wine
6 cups vegetable stock or water
1½ cups arborio rice
3 tablespoons fresh chopped
   Italian parsley
1 teaspoon dry thyme
Salt and freshly ground pepper

FRIED EGGS

4 tablespoons olive oil
   (more if needed)
4 or 6 fresh eggs
Salt and pepper

1 Melt butter or heat oil in a cast-iron saucepan. Keep heat to low-medium. Chop onion into small pieces and add to saucepan. Sauté lightly for 1 or 2 minutes, then add peas. Stir often.

2 Combine wine and water in another saucepan over medium heat. Keep it hot.

3 Add rice, parsley, and thyme to onion-pea combination and stir well for a few seconds. Add about half of the boiling wine-stock mixture to rice, and salt and pepper to taste. Stirring constantly, continue simmering until most of the liquid is absorbed. Add remaining stock liquid and stir intermittently. Cover rice until it's almost done. Stir often so rice doesn't stick at the bottom. When rice is done, it should be tender and the remaining liquid as thick as a sauce (very little will be left).

4 During the last minute the rice cooks, heat olive oil in a frying pan (about 4 tablespoons). When oil is hot, break 4 to 6 eggs into the pan, sprinkle the top with salt and pepper, and cover the frying pan for a second or two. Don't overcook eggs; they must remain moist.

5 When risotto is done, serve it in 4 or 6 serving dishes. Place one lightly fried egg on the top center of the risotto and serve immediately. The dish must be served and eaten while rice and eggs are hot. For a bit of extra taste, sprinkle grated Parmesan cheese on top.

TODAY IS THE SOLEMNITY of Saint Joseph, a saint very close to my heart. As I look forward to today's celebration, I thank the Lord for the beautiful day he has given us as we honor such a great, humble, and unique saint. The sun is shining gloriously in a blue, cloudless sky. The few inches of snow from the last couple of days have all but melted. A single breath of the cool, fresh spring air is intoxicating and, of course, the daffodils and early crocuses are showing their best throughout the monastic enclosure. It feels good to see spring get closer and closer. Winter has been long and harsh, a true test of our endurance. Spring is a most welcome change from winter's upheavals.

Since the Solemnity of Saint Joseph falls during Lent, today we're dispensed from the usual Lenten fast and can have two regular meals at the monastic table. One should be simple and the other more festive to honor the great Saint Joseph. There is a lot of joy in our kitchen as we plan the menu, for today we honor a saint who was a humble laborer and understood what daily work in the kitchen is all about. Indeed, in every facet of his life Saint Joseph is a unique model for monks and a saint with whom we can easily identify.

Every year as winter comes to a close, our cellar resources gradually diminish. So as I plan the menu, I check our winter cellar to see what vegetables are still solid and in good condition. Thank God squash, potatoes, and leeks are in a good state of preservation, and they will become the basis for a festive soup.

If a man's deeds are not in harmony with his prayer, he labors in vain.

ABBOT MOSES
DESERT FATHER

The wonderful thing about squash is that they have an impressively long shelf life. When kept in a cool cellar, most squash varieties can easily last four to six months and sometimes even longer. Some varieties actually become tastier and more flavorful with the passing of time. With this trio of survivors of our long winter, I can prepare an admirable first course.

SAINT JOSEPH LEEK, POTATO, AND SQUASH SOUP

6–8 SERVINGS

4 tablespoons butter
4 large leeks, well-washed,
   cut into thin slices, including
   some of the green parts
1 medium-size onion,
   coarsely chopped
2 garlic cloves, finely chopped
3 medium-size potatoes,
   peeled and cubed
1 good-size acorn squash
   (or butternut), peeled, halved,
   seeded, and cut into small chunks
9 cups vegetable stock or water
1 bunch of fresh parsley
   (about 6 sprigs), finely chopped
Salt and freshly ground pepper
¼ teaspoon nutmeg
1 cup heavy cream
A few parsley sprigs,
   finely chopped

1 In a large soup pot, melt butter over low-medium heat. Immediately add leeks, onion, and garlic. Stir continuously for 1 or 2 minutes. Turn off heat and add potatoes, squash, vegetable stock or water, and parsley. Reheat soup to medium-high and bring to a quick boil.

2 Allow to boil for about 5 minutes and then lower heat to low-medium. Cover pot and simmer soup slowly for about 30 minutes (add more stock or water if needed). Stir from time to time. When soup is done, turn off heat and allow to cool.

3 Transfer soup to a food processor or blender and purée thoroughly. Transfer the puréed soup back into the pot. Add salt and pepper to taste, nutmeg, and heavy cream. Mix well and reheat soup, stirring continuously or at least often. Serve soup hot and place some finely chopped parsley as garnish on each serving.

Since we're already gathering fresh eggs from our hens, our main course will consist of an egg-and-cheese dish that is a bit more attractive than the more ordinary ones of our Lenten diet. After a long winter's rest, our chickens have again started laying eggs. These fresh eggs are a great contribution to our monastic diet. We also use them to prepare desserts on special days.

Our main course for today is a zucchini soufflé, one of my favorite dishes be it winter, spring, summer, or fall. It's always a most attractive main course. It's accompanied by a rustic salad made of Belgian endives that can be eaten along with the soufflé or, better yet, right after.

SAINT JOSEPH ZUCCHINI SOUFFLÉ

4–6 SERVINGS

5 medium-size zucchini
3 shallots or one
    medium-size onion,
    minced
3 tablespoons butter
5 eggs, separated
½ cup, 4 tablespoons
    grated Parmesan
    cheese

BÉCHAMEL SAUCE
3 tablespoons butter
3 tablespoons cornstarch
1½ cup milk
Nutmeg, salt, and pepper

1 Shred zucchini into a large bowl and sprinkle salt on top. Stir and set aside for about ½ hour. Drain zucchini, rinse with cold water, drain again, and squeeze out remaining liquid with your hands. Set aside.

2 Put minced shallots or onions and 3 tablespoons of butter in a frying pan and butter and sauté lightly over low-medium heat for about 2 minutes. Add zucchini and continue sautéing for another 2 to 3 minutes or until zucchini begin to brown.

3 Prepare béchamel sauce: Melt 3 tablespoons butter in a good-size saucepan over low heat. In a large cup, mix cornstarch with milk and stir until mixed. Add this mixture to saucepan and stir continuously. Add a dash of nutmeg, salt, and pepper to taste and continue stirring until mixture becomes creamy and smooth. Set aside.

4 Preheat oven to 350° F. Beat egg yolks in a deep bowl with a mixer. Add ½ cup grated Parmesan and zucchini mixture. Mix well. Add béchamel sauce and gently mix well.

5 In another large bowl, beat the egg whites with mixer until stiff. Gently stir about ½ of the stiff egg whites into the zucchini mixture and fold lightly.

6 Butter a good-size soufflé dish thoroughly. Sprinkle the remaining Parmesan cheese in dish until the dish is well and evenly coated. Gently pour egg-zucchini mixture into the soufflé dish. Add the remaining stiff egg whites and again fold gently. Place soufflé in oven and bake for 20 to 25 minutes or until the soufflé is puffed and the top turns golden. Serve soufflé immediately after it comes out of the oven before it falls.

Today's dessert is a simple yet delicious dish originally from Spain that's also common throughout the south of France—a wonderful combination of poached figs in sweet sherry. I love figs in any shape or form of cooking, and for Saint Joseph's day I cannot think of anything better for dessert than a special dish of figs. (I usually use fresh figs to make this dessert, but on occasion I've resorted to dried figs, which turn out just as well.)

SAINT JOSEPH POACHED FIGS IN SHERRY WINE

6 SERVINGS

1 cup sweet sherry wine
1 cup water
1 strip of lemon zest
½ cup sugar, organic brown or white
¼ vanilla bean
1 cinnamon stick
Dash of nutmeg
18 fresh figs
6 tablespoons crème fraîche
　or vanilla yogurt

1 In a saucepan, combine sherry wine (good quality is preferable), water, lemon zest, sugar, vanilla bean, cinnamon stick, and nutmeg. Bring to a boil over medium–high heat and cook for about 5 minutes. Reduce heat to low–medium.

2 Add figs to sherry sauce and cook slowly until they are tender yet intact. The cooking process should not be more than 25 minutes. When figs are done, transfer them to a serving bowl.

3 Serve this dessert at room temperature, though it can also be refrigerated and served cold during the warm-weather months. Serve 4 figs and some of the poaching liquid per serving, topping it with a tablespoon of crème fraîche or vanilla yogurt as garnish.

OCCASIONALLY READERS ASK for Lenten menu suggestions. They maintain that in our hectic, mechanized age, it's very difficult to keep a Lenten diet that is both nourishing and frugal.

In today's culture, often both parents have worked all day and arrive home tired, and there isn't much time left before dinner. For some, it's simpler just to order a pizza. A pizza once in a while isn't too bad as long as its preceded by a wholesome soup or accompanied by a healthy salad. But doing that every day is another story.

The secret to solving this problem is to plan ahead and measure properly how much time, realistically speaking, you have for preparation of a meal. Some things—casseroles, for instance—can be prepared ahead of time, frozen, and served later in the week. Soups can be made in sufficient quantities and reheated and served over the following days.

The secret of a good recipe is not only in its ingredients, but also in the preparation demanded. When selecting recipes for the weekday table, choose simpler, lighter dishes that taste good and are nourishing but aren't complicated and don't take a long time to prepare or cook.

Here are plain and simple recipes particularly appropriate for Lent because of their frugality. They're also in the quick range, with preparation and cooking time of 30 to 45 minutes.

The right food always comes at the right time. Reliance on out-of-season foods makes the gastronomic year an endlessly boring repetition.

ROY ANDRIES DE GROOT

QUICK AND EASY EGGPLANT DISH

4 SERVINGS

6 tablespoons olive oil

1 large eggplant, washed and dried,
    peeled and cubed

1 good-size zucchini, sliced

1 red pepper, cut in thin long strips

1 medium-size Vidalia onion,
    coarsely chopped

1½ cups cherry tomatoes,
    washed and dried

A few leaves of fresh or dried basil,
    finely chopped

One dried bay leaf,
    whole or shredded

Salt and pepper

1 Pour olive oil into a deep skillet, add eggplant, zucchini, pepper, and onion. Sauté lightly over low-medium heat for 4 to 5 minutes. Stir constantly. Cover the skillet, reduce heat to low, and cook for about 5 more minutes or until the vegetables are tender.

2 Add tomatoes, basil, bay leaf, salt, and pepper and continue cooking for another 4 or 5 minutes. Serve vegetables hot over plain rice or a bed of egg noodles or spaghetti, which can be cooking (follow package directions) while vegetables are being prepared.

BROCCOLI, CAULIFLOWER, AND CHEESE CASSEROLE

6 SERVINGS

2 medium-size heads broccoli

2 medium-size heads cauliflower

4 eggs, beaten

1 cup ricotta cheese

½ cup grated cheddar cheese

1 tablespoon cornstarch,
    diluted in ⅔ cup milk

1 medium-size onion,
    finely chopped

Salt and freshly ground
    black pepper

1 Preheat oven to 350° F. Boil broccoli and cauliflower heads in salted water for about 10 minutes. Be sure the pot is covered, as it will help cook faster. Drain vegetables thoroughly and then chop them coarsely, including the stems. Set them aside.

2 Beat eggs in a deep bowl, add ricotta and cheddar cheese, cornstarch mixture, chopped onion, salt, and pepper. Mix thoroughly until ingredients are well blended.

3 Thoroughly butter an ovenproof elongated baking dish and place broccoli-cauliflower mixture in it. Bake for about 30 minutes. Serve hot accompanied by a plain dish of potatoes or rice.

POLPETTONE (Green Bean and Potato Casserole)

6 SERVINGS

1 pound green beans,
    fresh or frozen, trimmed
1 pound potatoes, peeled and diced
⅓ cup milk
6 eggs
½ cup grated Parmesan cheese
4 tablespoons olive oil
4 garlic cloves, minced
A few fresh parsley sprigs,
    finely chopped
1 tablespoon dried thyme
Salt and freshly ground black pepper
Olive oil or butter
½ cup bread crumbs
Butter

1 Boil green beans 12 to 15 minutes until tender. In a separate pot, boil potatoes in salted water for another 12 to 15 minutes or until cooked. Drain both vegetables and purée them together in a food processor or blender with milk. Add eggs one at a time and continue blending. Add Parmesan cheese and mix until ingredients are well blended. Set aside.

2 Heat olive oil in a small skillet and lightly sauté garlic, parsley, and thyme for about 1 minute. Stir continuously. Add garlic-herb mixture to bean-potato mixture. Add salt and pepper to taste and blend well.

3 Thoroughly oil or butter an elongated, shallow baking dish. Sprinkle bread crumbs over oil or butter until evenly covered. Add the bean-potato mixture and spread it evenly with a spatula. Cover with the remaining bread crumbs and dot with butter. Bake in a preheated oven at 350° F for 30 to 40 minutes or until puffed and the top turns golden. Serve hot.

*J*ANUARY AND FEBRUARY have come and gone, and March's end is almost here. Not everything is fun and lovely during the cold weather months: on some days, even a cozy fire brings only small comfort. Winter in the northeast tends to be long and bleak, and I know quite a few people for whom the long winter is a source of depression. This is why the approach of spring is looked on with such hope and anticipation. It's as if life were beginning all over again, filled with new expectation, new vitality, new incentives. Now spring has finally arrived, at least officially. The new season is a recurring theme of conversation among our local farmers and friends. Everyone seems to be smiling these days, for the brightness of spring indeed rejoices in the hearts of many in our midst.

But our joy today is not only about the arrival of the clear, wonderful days of spring. Today is a unique day in the Christian calendar, for we celebrate the Solemnity of the Annunciation, the feast that commemorates the great mystery of the Incarnation of the Son of God.

Our faith tells us the Incarnation began at the precise moment—the fullness of time as the Scriptures describe it—when Mary uttered her *fiat* in complete submission to the plan of God. Mary, of course, was familiar with the words of the prophet Isaiah: "Look, the young woman is with child and shall bear a son, and shall name him Immanuel" (7:14). What Mary hadn't known until that moment was that Isaiah was speaking of her, the woman eternally destined to bear the Father's only begotten Son. At the Annunciation, the archangel Gabriel stood amazed before the humble maiden from Nazareth and in a few chosen words declared, "Do not be afraid, Mary, for you have found favor with God. And now, you will conceive in your womb and bear a son, and you will name him Jesus" (Luke 1:30–31). At that very moment, by the power of God, the great mystery was accomplished: God, the author of all life, took human flesh from a lowly maiden. Nothing would ever be the same.

As far as I'm concerned, during Lent we exercise two kinds of cooking. The distinction is not so much about what is more or less nourishing, but more about the types of food and the quantities consumed during the fast. Basically, ordinary Lenten fare tends to be simple, frugal, and served in lower quantity. On the other hand, we have festivities such as today's, which falls during the Lenten fast but to which fasting rules don't apply. The fast is simply dispensed with.

Lenten food prepared at the monastery tends to be very basic and simple. It's

The best way to learn to cook is to cook: stand yourself in front of the stove and start right in.

JULIE DANNENBAUM
COOKING TEACHER

49

rather informal and inconsequential in many ways. Not many activities take place in the kitchen during the fast, just a bare minimum to adequately feed the monastic community.

On a feast day, however, the menu changes radically—more preparation, concentration, and more advance planning. This is just as it should be. During the days of the long Lenten journey, we need certain days to serve as sort of rest, and this is particularly expressed in the food we consume on such occasions. Today's meal will be our last festive one until Easter, for we still have two and half weeks before we complete the journey!

The first course for today's festive menu is a Swiss chard soup. We still have quite a bit of it in the freezer from the last harvest. Since the frozen Swiss chard is already partially cooked, it makes our kitchen labor much easier. If you don't have frozen Swiss chard, use some fresh from the garden or market or substitute the same amount of spinach.

SWISS CHARD SOUP

6–8 SERVINGS

1 large bunch of Swiss chard, frozen or fresh
3 leeks, washed and cleaned, thinly sliced (include tender green parts)
8 cups vegetable broth or water
2 egg yolks, well beaten (use mixer if necessary)
½ cup light cream
½ cup grated Parmesan cheese
Dash of nutmeg
Salt and freshly ground pepper
Bowl of grated Parmesan cheese

1 Chop Swiss chard coarsely (if frozen, allow it to defrost first). Place chard in a large soup pot. Add sliced leeks and broth or water. Cook over medium heat for 12 to 15 minutes or until vegetables are tender. Allow soup to cool a bit, and then pass it through a blender.

2 Reheat soup over low-medium heat. In a deep bowl, beat eggs well, add cream and Parmesan cheese, and blend ingredients well. Add mixture to soup and stir continuously.

3 Add nutmeg, salt, and pepper and continue stirring until soup is close to boiling point. *Do not allow to boil because cream and eggs will curdle.* Serve soup hot and pass bowl of Parmesan cheese to be sprinkled over soup as garnish.

Tonight's menu—a mushroom tart, a special salad, and crème brûlée—honors Jesus. By coming among us "eating and drinking" and taking great joy in meals with his friends and disciples, Jesus showed how deeply he embraced our humanity.

To prepare a tart, start with the basic dough, which in French is called la pâte brisée. *If you're short on time, don't hesitate to use a frozen prepared crust from the supermarkets.*

FINE DOUGH FOR TARTS AND QUICHES 1 6-SERVING TART OR QUICHE

1 egg
1 cup flour (if desired, mix half white
    and half whole-wheat flour)
1 stick butter or margarine
5 tablespoons ice water
Pinch of salt

1 Mix ingredients in a large bowl. Use both a fork and your hands for mixing. Do not overwork dough. Form a ball with the dough and sprinkle it with flour. Place dough in refrigerator for 1 hour to rest.

2 After 1 hour, sprinkle flour over the table or a board and carefully roll out dough, extending it in every direction. Butter a tart or pie dish thoroughly and place the rolled dough into it carefully. Dough must always be handled with the fingers. Trim the edges in a decorative fashion (French style).

3 Optional (but highly recommended for good baking): Cover pastry shell with aluminum foil and place in a 250° F oven for about 10 minutes for a prebaking period.

TARTE AUX CHAMPIGNONS (Mushroom Tart) 6 SERVINGS

3 tablespoons butter
1 medium-size onion, coarsely chopped
3 sprigs fresh parsley, finely chopped
½ teaspoon dried thyme
1 pound fresh mushrooms, thinly sliced
3 tablespoons dry white wine
3 eggs, beaten
1 cup heavy cream or half-and-half
Salt and freshly ground pepper
1 partially baked pie shell,
    prepared ahead of time

1 Melt butter in a good-size frying pan, add onions, parsley, and thyme. Sauté lightly over low-medium heat for about 2 minutes. Stir often. Add mushrooms and continue cooking for another 5 minutes. Add wine and raise heat to medium. Cook until wine evaporates.

2 Beat eggs in a deep bowl. Add cream, salt, and pepper and mix well. Add mushroom mixture and stir well. Carefully pour egg-mushroom mixture into prebaked tart shell. Bake in a preheated 350° F degree oven for 30 to 40 minutes or until the tart is done and puffed.

ANNUNCIATION DAY SALAD

6–8 SERVINGS

**1 medium-size head tender and
crisp endive, washed, leaves
trimmed and separated**
**1 small red onion, peeled and thinly
sliced in half moons**
2 firm yellow pears, cored and diced
5 tablespoons extra-virgin olive oil
4 tablespoons chopped walnuts
4 teaspoons red-wine vinegar
Salt and freshly ground pepper

1 Place endive leaves into a deep salad bowl.
Add onion and pears. Toss lightly.

2 Heat oil in skillet and add walnuts. Cook and stir until
walnuts turn light brown. Add vinegar and mix well.
Remove from heat, cool for 1 or 2 minutes, and then
pour mixture over salad. Add salt and pepper to taste and
toss again until all ingredients are evenly coated. Serve
immediately, either as an accompaniment to mushroom
tart or right after the tart and just before dessert.

CRÈME BRÛLÉE

4–6 SERVINGS

⅓ cup sugar
¼ cup boiling water
1 tablespoon cornstarch
2 cups milk
4 egg yolks
1 tablespoon cognac
1 small piece of lemon rind
1 teaspoon vanilla extract

1 Heat sugar in medium or large frying pan until it
begins to caramelize. Add water immediately and stir
continuously until mixture becomes a syrup.

2 In a cup, thoroughly mix cornstarch and 5 tablespoons
of milk. Scald the rest of the milk.

3 Beat egg yolks with a mixer and place them in
a double boiler filled with already-boiling water.
Immediately add cornstarch mixture, then gradually add
scalded milk and continue to stir. Slowly add caramel
syrup, lemon rind, cognac, and vanilla. Continue stirring
and cooking the cream over the boiling water until it
thickens. Remove cream from heat, discard lemon rind,
pour cream into individual dessert dishes (small ramekins
if you have them), and chill in the refrigerator for a few
hours until ready to be served at the table. Serve cold.

APRIL

*T*HE FIRST DAYS of April are full of surprises. Spring progresses slowly, at its own pace. Today is a typically windy spring day, with sunshine and clear skies and the joyful sound of blue jays calling to each other in earnest. The air smells refreshing and intoxicating. A clump of snowdrops surrounds Our Lady's statue, and the crocuses continue to multiply.

As the season moves forward, it demands a bit of patience from all of us. On the days we allocate to working outdoors and cleaning the debris in the garden, we're often interrupted by the uncertain weather. Some days it just rains too much for us to accomplish anything in the garden.

Spring's arrival is always a challenge because seasonal activities begin to multiply by the minute. I'm particularly happy when Daylight Savings Time arrives in early April because the demands of country life are many at this time of the year. Without that extra daylight, it would be very difficult to cope with both garden and kitchen work as well as the traditional spring urges to clean and fix everything.

Our long annual Lenten pilgrimage is nearly complete, and we're at the threshold of Holy Week. For Christians, this blessed time of Lent asserts that new life rises out of ashes and that our hope for an eternal spring is rooted in the promise of the resurrection. During these last Lenten days, no matter what the accomplishments of our Lenten observance, we must continue to find God in the small details of the daily: cooking, cleaning, gardening, washing, toiling, singing, praying, writing, painting, organizing daily chores, reading, and resting. Daily life is a series of endless details to enjoy and bring to fruition. Nothing is so small that it's not worthy of our care and attention, for ultimately we encounter the Lord in these tiny details of daily living. Through each, his presence shines and is revealed.

In the days approaching Holy Week, our fasting intensifies and our food consumption is reduced to our individual capacities. I'm often asked why we fast during Lent and Holy Week. Is it an act of masochism? No. Many good and healthy reasons exist for fasting. When people fast for other reasons, like to reduce weight and improve their figures, no one questions their motives. The body and soul also need training, daily exercise, and even a bit of self-denial for the sake of our own spiritual health. Besides, cutting back the quantity of food we eat doesn't mean going without.

But how about the real reasons for fasting at this time? During Lent and Holy Week, Christians contemplate the suffering Christ endured for our sake, and the bit of fasting we do during these days is a way of participating and sharing in the

*From you
I have been absent
in the spring,
When proud-pied
April dressed
in all his trim,
Hath put a
spirit of youth
in everything.*

SHAKESPEARE

mystery of that immense sacrifice. They say love tends to make people equal and ready to imitate the beloved. In our case, we try to follow Jesus even to the last steps in Calvary. Our fasting and self-denial are ways of accompanying the Master and sharing, in a very small way, in those painful last moments.

Another reason for fasting is that the Christian monk always wishes to live in some sort of solidarity with all God's children around the world, especially with the poor and suffering. Fasting is a great way of remembering the pain and need of others, and it makes me more appreciative of the good food consumed on other occasions. Fasting, when guided by faith and creatively pursued, can provide new vigor and energy to all aspects of our daily existence.

During these days of the great fast, our daily fare centers around a variety of nutritious soups. Tonight's soup is a basic one that has been consumed throughout the centuries in Portugal. They add Portuguese chorizo to the soup, making it a succulent dish. We omit the chorizo or meat part, creating a rather frugal soup that is well appropriate for Lent and Holy Week.

CALDO VERDE (Portuguese Soup With Cabbage

6 SERVINGS

10 cups water or vegetable stock
Pinch of sea salt
6 leeks, including the green parts
    that are tender and good,
    thinly sliced
1 small green cabbage,
    coarsely chopped
5 large potatoes, peeled and
    cubed
6 garlic cloves, minced
6 tablespoons olive oil,
    more if needed
Salt and freshly ground
    black pepper

1 In a large soup pot, bring water to a boil and add a pinch of salt. Lower heat to low-medium and add leeks, cabbage, and potatoes. Cover pot and continue boiling for 12 to 15 minutes.

2 Add garlic, olive oil, and salt and pepper to taste. Cover pot and allow soup to simmer over low to low-medium heat for 30 minutes. When soup is done, ladle into hot plates or bowls and serve hot. Serve fresh bread to accompany the soup. During the nonpenitential season, top the soup with freshly ground Parmesan or other cheese.

SOMETIMES I feel overwhelmed by the inner feelings spring arouses deep within me. Everything seems to be coming alive at once. Throughout the property, the forsythias show their early blooms and the daffodils display their glorious shades of yellow and white. All of nature seems to be in accord, breaking forth into a harmonious symphony of colors and sounds, attesting to the undeniable reality that spring is truly here.

In the northern hemisphere, the celebration of Holy Week and Easter always coincide with the arrival of spring. Our monastic life seems to become extra quiet during these days of Passiontide. A profound silence pervades the whole monastery. Even our farm animals seem calmer, more serene. And why not? The suffering of Christ, the Passion and death he endured and his glorious resurrection are cosmic events. The whole world is weeping as we see him, the innocent Lamb of God, going to the slaughter and being crucified for our sake.

Our monastic diet tends to be more austere during Holy Week—days of intense living and profound reflection and praying. All of our Lenten efforts seem to converge on this final dramatic week when we accompany Jesus to Calvary, to his Shabbat rest on Holy Saturday, and ultimately to the glory of Easter. During these special days, we plunge into deep prayer and mourning as we consume smaller amounts of very plain food, just enough to nourish us and give us that extra bit of energy to complete the journey. I call it "creative restraint."

A great deal of what we consume these days are simple, basic soups. Here are some recipes that throughout the years have become particularly useful to a monastery cook and most appropriate for these penitential days of Holy Week.

Spring is God thinking in gold, laughing in blue, and speaking in green.

FRANK JOHNSON

HOLY WEEK BREAD AND TOMATO SOUP

6–8 SERVINGS

⅔ cup olive oil

5 garlic cloves, minced

1 large Spanish onion, coarsely chopped

20 thin slices of stale French bread
   (or Italian), halved

6 tomatoes, peeled and seeded, coarsely
   chopped, or about 3 pounds of drained
   plum tomatoes

3 tablespoons dried or fresh rosemary,
   finely chopped

3 tablespoons dried or fresh sage, finely chopped

12 cups vegetable stock or water

1 cup dry white wine (optional)

Salt and freshly ground black pepper

1 Pour oil into a large soup pot over low-medium heat. Add garlic and onion. Sauté for about 1 minute, stirring continuously. Add bread, tomatoes, rosemary, and sage. Continue stirring for 5 minutes.

2 In a separate pot, bring the stock or water and wine to a boil. After the bread and tomatoes have sautéed for 5 minutes, pour the boiling stock or water into the soup pot (add more water if needed). Season with salt and pepper. Cover pot and simmer soup slowly over low-medium heat for about 40 minutes. Stir occasionally. Serve soup while it's still hot.

I enjoy preparing this next simple soup during Holy Week and all of early spring, taking advantage of the early sorrels we harvest in our herb garden. Those who don't cultivate sorrel may substitute it with wild sorrel that grows practically everywhere (smaller leaves, of course) in the countryside. You may substitute spinach; it won't taste the same, but it will be close.

SORREL-LEEK-POTATO SOUP

6–8 SERVINGS

6 tablespoons olive or vegetable oil
   or 4 tablespoons butter

3 leeks, thinly sliced, including
   tender green parts

4 potatoes, peeled and cubed

8 cups vegetable stock or water

6 cups fresh sorrel (cultivated
   or wild), coarsely chopped

Salt and white pepper

1 cup milk

½ cup sour cream

1 Pour oil or melt butter in a large soup pot. Add leeks and sauté over low-medium heat for 3 to 5 minutes. Add potatoes and stock or water and bring to a quick boil over medium-high heat. Reduce heat to low-medium and add sorrel, milk, salt, and pepper. Stir well and let soup simmer gently for about 30 minutes. Stir occasionally.

2 When soup is done, allow it to cool for a few minutes. Add milk and stir well. Working in batches, blend soup in a food processor or blender and purée until soup turns creamy and smooth. Reheat soup in a clean pot, but don't bring it to a boil. Serve soup hot in preheated plates or bowls, and top each with a full tablespoon of sour cream in the center.

Easter

TODAY we celebrate Easter, the day Christians around the world commemorate the Lord's glorious resurrection from the dead. Easter has been the goal of our Lenten journey, the joyful reward for our Lenten struggles, the fulfillment of our hope. The resurrection of Christ means God's triumph over the powers of darkness: Our sins have been nailed to the cross and thus washed away by the immense love Christ showed for us at the moment of his death.

As we celebrate Easter, we're reminded of what is really important in life. Our relationship with God is the most vital and essential element in our lives. How we love and care for each other flows directly from our closeness to God.

The resurrection of Christ is also the titular feast of our small monastery and thus a day of great rejoicing. For people living in the northern hemisphere, this paschal feast coincides with the arrival of spring, a magical season filled with hope and promise. During these early spring days, we witness the clothing of our trees with new foliage and the marvel of the earth's renewal all around us. How perfectly appropriate that the inner renewal brought to us by the Easter grace should coincide with the visible renewal taking place in our universe.

This pleasant Easter morning, we rose to sing Lauds later than usual. It was the right thing to do after the beautiful but long Easter Vigil we kept last night. Our tired bodies always tell us when we need that extra bit of blessed rest. As is our custom on Christmas and Easter, a lovely bowl of hot chocolate with warm croissants awaited us at breakfast. Our monastic customs enhance the celebration of holy days and make them extra special.

I must rush a bit this morning. Today's menu must somehow reflect the character of the feast and the joy we all feel in the glory of the resurrection. I've planned the menu well ahead to make sure it's both festive and practical on a day when I don't have much time to spend in the kitchen. On days like today, our Offices are extra long and much time is devoted to prayer, singing, and contemplation.

The appetizer will be simple: fresh melon with yogurt and a touch of mint. For the main course, I've planned a dish of crepes filled with Swiss chard, cheese, and hard-boiled eggs. Crepes are great for festive meals because they're easy to make and can be filled with almost anything: a simple ratatouille, ham and cheese, Swiss chard or spinach, and hard-boiled eggs. Crepes also make wonderful desserts and again, depending on the fruit filling, the varieties are endless.

The crepes for today's meal were made yesterday and refrigerated, so all I have to

Hail, O noble festival Day! Blessed day that is holy forever. Day wherein God conquered death, and Christ arose from the tomb.

SALVE FESTA DIES,
VENANTIUS FORTUNATUS
(D. 609)

do today is warm them, shape the fillings, pour heavy cream or half-and-half over them to keep them moist, and place them in the oven. The cream or half-and-half is better than any sauce or other tricks.

After the main course, a crunchy salad with a good chevre will follow, topped off with a fruit-and-custard dessert.

Although a good meal is essential to today's celebration, I don't plan to spend the whole day in the kitchen. I need extra time for quiet prayer, to walk in the fields, and to play with our farm animals, especially the newborn lambs. Christ is Risen, Alleluia, Alleluia!

MELON WITH YOGURT AND FRESH MINT

6 SERVINGS

3 small ripe melons
4 tablespoons lemon juice
One 16-ounce container
    low-fat plain yogurt
Salt and freshly ground black pepper
A few fresh mint leaves,
    finely chopped and minced

1 Cut each melon into two equal parts. Clean the insides and discard seeds. Sprinkle lemon juice over each half.

2 Place yogurt in a bowl, add remaining lemon juice, salt, pepper, and part of the finely chopped mint and mix well. Refrigerate until chilled.

3 Just before serving, fill each melon hollow with the yogurt mixtures. Sprinkle the remaining chopped mint on each melon. Serve cold.

CREPES WITH SWISS CHARD–CHEESE FILLING

CREPES

4 eggs

2 tablespoons vegetable oil

1¼ cups flour

Pinch of salt

4 cups milk

Melted butter or oil

(Note: Crepes can be made a day ahead and kept covered in the refrigerator.)

SWISS CHARD FILLING

2 tablespoons butter

1 onion, chopped

1 pound fresh Swiss chard, washed, cooked, and chopped

4 hard-boiled eggs, chopped

Salt and pepper

8 slices of Gruyère or Swiss cheese

OPTIONAL: 8 SLICES OF COOKED HAM; 1 CUP HEAVY CREAM

1 Put eggs, oil, flour, and salt into a large bowl. Beat with a whisk or an electric hand mixer. While beating, add milk one cup at a time. Batter should have the consistency of heavy cream and be free of lumps. If batter is too thick, add a teaspoon or two of cold water and continue to mix until it's light and smooth. Refrigerate batter for an hour or two before cooking crepes.

2 Heat a 6- or 8-inch skillet over a high flame and lightly brush the entire surface with a bit of melted butter. Pour about ¼ cup of batter into skillet, swirling the batter until it covers the entire bottom of the pan. Cook crepe for 1 to 1½ minutes or until it shows signs of turning brown around the edges. Flip crepe with a spatula and cook the other side for 1 minute. When crepe is done, slide it carefully onto a flat plate. Brush skillet once more with butter and repeat steps until all batter is used. Set crepes aside while you make the filling.

3 In a nonaluminum pan, melt 1 tablespoon of butter and sauté onion gently until it's translucent. Add Swiss chard, cook for 1 or 2 minutes, and then remove from heat. Add eggs and salt and pepper to taste; blend well.

4 Preheat oven to 300° F. Coat a 9-inch by 13-inch baking dish with the remaining tablespoon of butter. Put a slice of cheese on each crepe and, if you wish, a slice of ham. Add 2 heaping teaspoons of the Swiss chard mixture down the center of each crepe. Roll each crepe and place it carefully in the baking dish, seam-side down. Set crepes close together in the dish. Pour heavy cream over them and bake 15 to 20 minutes. Serve hot.

SALADE DE MESCLUN AVEC DE CHEVRE
(Provençal Mesclun Salad With Goat Cheese)
8 SERVINGS

1 pound tender mixed greens (mesclun)
1 small red onion, thinly sliced
6 slices goat cheese
6 sprigs of rosemary (or thyme)
Extra-virgin olive oil
6 slices French bread

VINAIGRETTE
8 tablespoons olive oil
3 tablespoons wine vinegar
1 teaspoon lemon juice
Salt and freshly ground pepper

1 Wash and rinse salad greens, dry well, and place in a bowl. Add sliced onion and toss gently.

2 Preheat oven to 350° F or preheat broiler. Place goat cheese (entire slice or crumbled) on each slice of bread. Sprinkle virgin olive oil on cheese and press a rosemary sprig into the cheese. Place bread in an oven-proof dish and put it in the oven or under the broiler until cheese bubbles and begins to melt.

3 Mix dressing ingredients well. Pour over salad. Toss salad and distribute evenly among six serving plates.

4 Place one cheese-bread slice at the center of each salad plate. Serve immediately.

PEARS BAKED IN CUSTARD
8 SERVINGS

4 large or 6 small ripe pears
1 cup milk
3 eggs
½ cup granulated sugar
1½ teaspoon cornstarch
2 tablespoons cognac or pear brandy or 1 teaspoon vanilla extract
Butter for baking dish
Nutmeg, preferably freshly grated
Confectioners' (powdered) sugar

Note: Pears can be halved or cut into thin slices.

1 Preheat oven to 350° F. Peel, halve, and core pears. Set aside. In a mixing bowl, whisk milk, eggs, sugar, cornstarch, and cognac until thoroughly blended.

2 Generously butter a large (9-inch by 13-inch or similar size) baking dish. Pour a thin layer of custard into dish and place dish in hot oven for 2 minutes or until custard sets. Remove dish from oven and arrange pears on custard. Sprinkle a little extra granulated sugar over the fruit if you wish. Pour the rest of the custard over fruit. Sprinkle lightly with nutmeg.

3 Bake on a rack in the center of the oven for about 40 minutes or until custard is set and starting to brown. Remove from oven and sprinkle with confectioners' (powdered) sugar. Serve warm.

"APRIL SHOWERS bring May flowers," says the old adage. It's true that during both March and April the constant rains test our endurance, but when I think of those magic tulips, hyacinths, and gorgeous scented lilacs that will brighten our May days, the rain becomes a small inconvenience. Besides, on rainy days like today I have more time for writing. Since I'm always behind, I bless the Lord for giving me this opportunity. Creative writing, almost as much as cooking and gardening, can bring so much joy and renewed energy into our personal lives. Sometimes writing is a burden. On those days I lay it aside. Other times, the hours of writing are hours of content and pure illumination.

One of the beautiful customs we keep in the monastery is the traditional blessing of food after the long Easter Vigil. In ancient times, after the long Lenten fast the Christians of Europe and the Middle East loved to break the penitential practice with a joyful celebration with family and fellow Christians. They usually carried to church a basket of the new Easter bread, hard-boiled eggs, cheeses, sausages, ham, new radishes, asparagus, and pastries and other sweets. At the end of the Easter liturgy, the food was blessed by the priest. Afterward, some of the food was consumed at the church and the rest carried home for the day's main meal.

Here in the monastery, at the conclusion of our Easter Liturgy we gather around the dining-room table, where all sorts of food are spread: eggs, cheese, bread, cakes, canapes, tapas, small sandwiches, herbs, mushrooms, fruits, olives, fruit juices, and wine. All are blessed, with each food having its own blessing. A tiny paschal lamb, usually the last born to our flock, is blessed as a reminder of Christ, our immolated Lamb of God. The lamb is led back to the barn as everyone partakes of the newly blessed food.

Some Gospel narratives relate how the risen Lord shared food and wine with his disciples on that Easter night, reminding us of the importance the Son of Man attached

Today all things are filled with light: therefore let the heavens rejoice and the earth be glad. For Christ is indeed risen from the dead, our source of true and endless joy!

BYZANTINE
PASCHAL CANON

to food. This lovely custom of blessing the food we consume at Easter, on the Feast of the Transfiguration, and before every meal is a reminder of the sacred character of food and its innate goodness. It's also a strong reminder of the immense generosity of God, who provides us daily with the good things of this earth.

Among the many small comestibles (finger-food) prepared for this year's traditional blessing of the food on the Paschal night are asparagus quiche, spinach-ham croquettes, fried cauliflower, stuffed eggs and, of course, the famous Easter bread called *Pascha*. Here are some of our paschal recipes.

ASPARAGUS QUICHE

10 TO 12 SMALL PIECES

1 egg
1 cup flour
1 stick sweet butter
    or margarine
5 tablespoons ice water
Pinch of salt

FILLING

1 pound fresh asparagus
4 medium eggs,
    lightly beaten
8 ounces Swiss cheese,
    cut into small pieces
⅔ cup half-and-half or
    heavy cream
3 fresh parsley sprigs,
    finely chopped
Salt and freshly
    ground pepper

1 Prepare pastry shell by mixing egg, flour, sweet butter or margarine, ice water, and salt in a deep bowl. Use both a fork and your hands to mix until dough forms. Don't overwork dough. Form the dough into a ball and sprinkle with flour. Refrigerate for at least 1 hour.

2 Sprinkle flour over your work surface and gently roll out the dough, extending it in every direction. Thoroughly butter a tart or quiche pan or 8-or 9-inch pie dish. Handling the dough only with your fingers, carefully place it in the pan. Trim dough edges in a decorative manner. Cover pastry shell with aluminum foil and place in the oven at 250° F for 10 to 12 minutes.

3 Trim and halve asparagus stems. Boil for about 5 minutes. Drain thoroughly, then dry with paper towel.

4 When pastry shell is done, raise oven temperature to 350° F. Beat eggs in a bowl. Add cheese, half-and-half or heavy cream, parsley, salt, and pepper, and blend until mixture is uniform throughout. Pour mixture into precooked tart or pie shell, smoothing evenly with a fork. Arrange asparagus tips on mixture in a sunburst shape, pointing out from the middle. Asparagus tips should be at the edge of the quiche. Place the rest of the asparagus in the empty spaces. Bake at 350 ° F for about 30 minutes. Serve hot or cold. To serve, slice carefully into small pieces.

CROQUETTES AUX EPINARDS AU FROMAGE
(Spinach Cheese Croquettes)

4 SERVINGS

1 onion, finely chopped
2 eggs
1 cup spinach, chopped and cooked
3 slices cooked ham, finely chopped
1 cup bread crumbs
1 tablespoon vegetable oil
1 teaspoon lemon juice
1 cup grated cheese
Salt and pepper
Vegetable oil
Flour

1 Lightly sauté diced onion. Beat one egg in a deep bowl. Add onion, cooked spinach (drained of all water), ham, and bread crumbs. Blend well. Add cheese, lemon juice, vegetable oil, salt, and pepper and mix thoroughly. Refrigerate for at least 1 hour.

2 Beat the other egg. Remove spinach mixture from refrigerator and form into small balls about 2½ inches wide. Dip balls into the beaten egg, and then roll them in flour. Deep fry them in vegetable oil until they turn golden brown. Drain them on a paper towel and serve hot.

PESTO-FILLED DEVILED EGGS

SERVES 10

10 hard-boiled eggs, peeled
⅓ cup olive oil, plus more for drizzling
3 large garlic cloves, peeled
12 leaves fresh basil
Salt and pepper

1 Halve hard–boiled eggs lengthwise. Carefully remove the egg yolks and place them in a bowl. Mash them with a fork.

2 Place olive oil, garlic, and basil leaves in a blender and whirl until smooth. Add salt and pepper to taste and blend again. Add this pesto to the mashed egg yolks and mix well. Fill egg whites with pesto mixture. Place stuffed egg halves on a large plate and serve.

FRIED CAULIFLOWER

8 SERVINGS

1 good-size
    cauliflower head
⅓ cup white flour
⅓ cup Parmesan cheese,
    grated
Salt and freshly
    ground pepper
1 egg, beaten
½ cup light beer
Vegetable oil

1 Place water in a large saucepan. Add a dash of salt and the cauliflower head and bring to a boil for 15 minutes or until it's cooked but still firm. Rinse and drain under cold water. Cut the florets carefully off the stalk, then halve florets.

2 Put flour into a medium-size bowl and add cheese, salt, and pepper. Mix well, then make a hole in the center. Pour beaten egg into the hole. Add beer gradually, and with a fork draw the rest of the ingredients into the liquid. Mix well and let stand for about 45 minutes.

3 Pour oil into a frying pan and heat to medium–high.
Dip about 3 pieces of cauliflower into the batter at a time, gently shaking off the excess batter before placing them in the frying pan. Fry cauliflower for about 3 minutes, making sure to fry it on both sides. Place a paper towel on a large plate. When cauliflower turns golden, remove carefully and put on the plate. The paper towel will help drain excess oil. When all florets are cooked, serve them at room temperature or, after removing paper towel, reheat them at 150° F for a few minutes before serving.

NCE THE PASCHAL FEAST is celebrated in the monastery, the natural fatigue felt throughout Lent comes to an end. As Easter is celebrated in joyful tones, we seem to be re-energized after enduring the long, harsh winter. We feel deeply grateful for the transition into spring, a season which happily coincides with our Paschal celebrations and serves as an inspiration to our labors. Country people, including the monks and nuns who are loving stewards to the land entrusted to them, start pining for good weather to work outdoors in the moment the first crocuses peek through the lingering snow.

Now that the late March–early April mud has almost all dried, the new greenery in our fields keeps getting taller and taller and is almost ready for the sheep. On a sunny day it's a lovely sight to see the mother ewes and newborn lambs enjoy the solace of the sun and the taste of the tender greens. And, of course, I enjoy the sweet "baahs" of their young cries. Our gardens are also in full bloom, showing a tantalizing display of colors and shapes: daffodils, tulips, anemones, Japanese irises, early pansies, and others. Truly, April and May are bulb months, since most of the plants in bloom are of bulb origin. To me, Eastertime and spring are one season of faith, hope, renewal, rebirth, and new life—and all of it because of the resurrection of Christ!

For the past week during breakfast, we have been steadily eating the bread baked and blessed during the paschal night. Most monasteries around the world are associated with their own bread recipes for holiday celebrations. Our own monastery has bread recipes for Advent, Christmas, Lent, and, of course, Easter. In many ways, each kind of bread is a symbol of both the season and, more important, of Christ himself, who told his disciples: "I am the bread of life" (John 6:48).

When Christmas and Easter arrive, I find nothing more gratifying than baking the breads consumed in the monastery during the holidays. Whether the recipe is plain or simple doesn't matter. What is important is the newness and freshness, the delight we experience crunching the new blessed bread, a real symbol of the spirit of the feast and season.

The following recipe is quick and simple, one anybody can bake at the last minute. I usually use round pans for baking the breads to be blessed after the Easter Vigil, but you can also use a rectangular loaf pan.

Anyone who has a bulb has spring.

ANONYMOUS

EASTER BREAD

2½ cups lukewarm water
1 package yeast
4 tablespoons honey
1 teaspoon salt
⅓ cup brown or white sugar
½ cup raisins
1¾ tablespoons shortening
4 cups white flour
4 cups whole-wheat flour

1 Dissolve yeast and honey in ½ cup lukewarm water. In a deep bowl or casserole, mix the rest of the water, salt, sugar, raisins, and shortening. Add yeast mixture, then gradually add flour.

2 Knead until dough turns smooth and flexible. Place dough in a greased bowl, cover with a towel, and set in a warm place to rise until it doubles in size. Punch down and let rise again.

3 Divide dough equally among 3 medium-size greased loaf pans. Let loaves rise until they double in size. Using a thin knife, make a cross in the center of each loaf. Preheat oven to 350° F, and then bake for about ½ hour.

*B*LESSING PRAYER FOR THE EASTER BREAD

Lord Jesus Christ, our God and risen Savior,
You are the bread of angels, the bread that gives eternal life.
For our sake you came down from heaven
and fed us with the spiritual food of your divine gifts.
Bless this bread and the food at this table
as you once blessed the five loaves in the wilderness.
Bless all those who will partake of it.
May this blessed bread and food be a source
of bodily and spiritual health for all who eat them.
For you are all holy, and to you we give glory,
together with the Father and the Holy Spirit,
now and forever and ever. Amen.

OUR FENCED-IN GARDEN, rustic in its monastic simplicity, has been a place of solace and joy, a boundary within which vegetables, flowers and herbs grow happily together and produce plenty under the close scrutiny and protection of Saint Fiacre, the monk and patron saint of gardeners. Weather permitting, we spend the last days of April in intense garden work: removing winter debris, raking leaves from garden paths, preparing beds for the planting, repairing garden fences and damaged raised beds, testing soils, adding compost to the beds, and planting the early seedlings. We earn plenty of sweat equity in our endeavors, and it will repay us at the end of the season with an abundance of marvelous fresh organic produce.

While working in the garden today, my thoughts are also directed toward the kitchen. What do I envision for the evening meal on a day of heavy activity outdoors, when little time is left for indoor chores like cooking? Rice readily comes to my mind. Rice is a good thing at any time of the year. Besides, I like to experiment and improvise with rice. This magic grain lends itself to many creations and transformations in our humble monastery kitchen. Throughout the years I've developed not only a deep affinity for rice, but also a very healthy respect for this humble staple.

Rice is one of the most popular grains in world's cuisine. It's rich in iron, zinc, and vitamin B and has plenty of folic acid. From the cultural point of view, rice has always been an integral part of the basic Mediterranean diet and thus the diet of Christian monasteries in that part of the world, much as it has been part of the diet of Zen monks in Japan and the rest of Asia.

Rice is claimed to have been first introduced to southern Europe, France, Spain, and Italy by the Saracens, the Moslem population who invaded that region of Europe. In Italy the humble staple received the name *risotto*, while in France it was called *riz* and in Spain *arroz*. In those countries rice is held in high esteem to this day, which means it's served separately instead of as a side dish as we do in the United States. Rice

The way one eats is the way one works.

CZECH PROVERB

68

is a handy and versatile grain that can accompany any meat, vegetable, fish, or egg dish.

I often prepare rice in the monastery. When caught in a dilemma at the last minute about what to serve with any vegetable or fish, I always reach for a cup of rice because I know the result will be agreeable to both the eyes and the palate.

As we wind down the last days of April and prepare to move into May, I like to concentrate my cooking skills on several rice dishes that stretch the whole range from soups to dessert. I use different brands and varieties of rice in our daily cooking, but I do have a predilection for arborio rice, which is *de rigueur* in Italian dishes that require rice. The exquisite thing about arborio rice is the creamy texture it produces while remaining *al dente*.

Tonight's menu is a hearty dish of rice with lentils, Mediterranean style, followed by a plain green salad and some leftover pear compote as dessert. An added benefit is the combination of lentils and rice, which renders the complete protein necessary in our daily diet.

LENTIL RISOTTO

6–8 SERVINGS

1½ cups small lentils (French style)
4 tablespoons olive oil
4 garlic cloves, minced
1 medium-size onion,
    coarsely chopped
1 celery stalk, thinly sliced
2 tablespoons dry thyme
1 bay leaf
4 plum tomatoes, seeded and
    coarsely chopped
Salt and freshly ground pepper
1½ cups arborio or other rice
2 tablespoons butter
¾ cup grated Parmesan or
    pecorino Romano cheese

1 Soak lentils for about 4 hours and then drain. Cook lentils in 5 to 6 cups salted boiling water for 5 minutes. Cover pot, reduce heat to low, and simmer for 30 to 40 minutes until tender.

2 Heat oil in a good-size saucepan. Add garlic, onion, celery, thyme, and bay leaf. Sauté lightly over low-medium heat 4 to 5 minutes. Stir often. Add tomatoes, raise heat to medium, and continue cooking another 8 to 10 minutes or until it turns into an even sauce. Add lentils with remaining water, then salt and pepper to taste. Add rice and stir. Cover and simmer over low-medium heat for another 8 to 10 minutes or until rice is tender and most of the liquid evaporates. Remove bay leaf. Add butter and grated cheese. Stir gently and serve. Optional: Serve grated cheese separately at the table to top the rice-lentil dish.

When I prepare a rice dish as a main course, I often cook extra rice for use the next day in preparing rice croquettes or tortillitas de arroz. *Together they're a great accompaniment to any vegetable dish or salad; alone, they make a delicious light supper.*

MONASTERY RICE CROQUETTES

ABOUT 6 SERVINGS

3 tablespoons olive oil
2 garlic cloves, minced
3 parsley sprigs, finely chopped
½ teaspoons dry thyme
½ pound mushrooms,
  coarsely chopped
3 cups cooked rice
2 eggs
Salt and freshly ground pepper
⅓ cup grated Parmesan or
  mozzarella cheese,
  finely chopped
Whole wheat flour
Bread crumbs
Vegetable or olive oil

1 Pour 3 tablespoons of olive oil in a frying pan and gently cook garlic, parsley, and thyme for 1 minute. Stir continuously. Add mushrooms and continue cooking over low-medium heat 4 to 5 minutes. Set aside to cool for a few minutes.

2 In a large mixing bowl, place rice and 1 egg. Salt and pepper to taste. Mix well. Moisten your hands with cold water. Shape rice mixture into 3-inch-diameter balls. Use your finger to punch a hole in the center of each ball and place a teaspoon of the mushroom mixture and an even smaller amount of the cheese (Parmesan or chopped mozzarella) into each hole. Cover the hole with rice until it's completely closed.

3 Roll croquettes in whole-wheat flour, dip them in one well-beaten egg, and roll them in bread crumbs. Deep fry croquettes in hot oil until all sides turn crisp and golden. Serve hot.

MAY

MAY 1 ◆ Saint Joseph the Worker

MAY IS THE TIME OF YEAR when the apple orchards in the Hudson Valley display all their glory. Just before the trees bloom, the subtle misty grays and tender greens begin to appear in their new foliage. Today is a cool, moist, cloudless spring day, one of those days early in the season when one delights in quietly working in the garden. Today we also keep the memory of Saint Joseph the Worker, a model for monks and laborers of all times and seasons. Saint Joseph was robust and strong and not afraid to give himself completely to his carpentry to support the Holy Family entrusted to him.

One of the tragedies of our time is the way we malign manual labor and those who perform it, whether they be the humble migrant who roams the countryside, the factory laborer, the cleaning crew in our homes and offices, or the quiet craft worker, all doing what they know how to do. How can we not show respect for them and their trade when we depend so much on their help? I keep thinking about Saint Joseph, the lowly carpenter, while I continue my garden tasks. My heart lifts in thanksgiving to God for that very special grace given to monks to be able to live from the work of our hands as Saint Joseph did and as Saint Benedict prescribes in his book *The Rule of Saint Benedict*. Manual labor, when performed in quiet and with human dignity, helps monks remain grounded in reality, in humility, in solidarity with other workers. It is indeed a source of many blessings and a reason for our inner contentment.

Several years ago a young man who made retreats at our monastery spent the summer in France. He said the monastery gardens cultivated and lovingly cared for by the monks and nuns had impressed him more than anything else he'd seen on his trip. "There is real life in the gardens," he told me. "You can almost feel the pulse of the monks' life by the work you see accomplished there."

This comment made me stop and reflect on the history, the purpose, and the importance attached to gardens in the daily life of a monastery. Monastic gardening is as ancient as monastic life itself. Through the ages, monks and nuns have held fast to the biblical story that God created "the man and put him in the garden of Eden to till it

They are truly monks when they live by the labor of their hands, as did our fathers and the Apostles.

THE RULE OF SAINT BENEDICT

and keep it" (Genesis 2:15). From the beginnings of monastic life in the Egyptian desert, garden work was acknowledged as part of God's command to care for the earth. The lives and writings of those early monks and nuns show them to be efficient and avid gardeners. Since their gardens had to be cultivated under difficult circumstances on desert soil, the monks patiently and with great wisdom went about developing the principles of monastic gardening that would be followed by monks for centuries to come.

This afternoon, while heavily involved in garden work, I begin to plan tonight's supper. A friend of the monastery, a local farmer, dropped by earlier with some lovely asparagus, and I decide to construct a simple dish around it. During these busy days of early planting, the daily garden work absorbs me, cutting down on some of the time I spend preparing the evening dinner. Part of being both a gardener and a cook entails trying to use time wisely.

A COMPLETE SPRING SALAD
4 SERVINGS

20 fresh asparagus spears, trimmed,
    lightly boiled or steamed
8 small-to-medium potatoes, peeled,
    boiled in salted water, evenly sliced
4 hard-boiled eggs, peeled and
    halved lengthwise
24 cherry tomatoes, washed and dried
20 black or green olives, whole or seeded

ROSEMARY-SCENTED VINAIGRETTE
8 tablespoons extra-virgin olive oil
6 teaspoons red-wine vinegar or lemon juice
1 teaspoon Dijon mustard
Salt and freshly ground black pepper
1 sprig of greens from a rosemary branch,
    pounded and finely chopped

1 Arrange on each plate in decorative order 5 asparagus spears, 2 sliced potatoes, 1 egg sliced in halves, 6 cherry tomatoes, and 5 olives.

2 Prepare vinaigrette ahead of time so the rosemary can infuse it. Combine vinaigrette ingredients and whisk well. Just before serving, pour a small amount of vinaigrette over asparagus, potatoes, and eggs. Serve immediately at room temperature.

3 This salad is a complete meal in itself. A piece of fruit or light dessert is all one needs afterward.

OPTIONAL: TO SERVE AS A DELICIOUS POTATO SALAD, CHOP AND COMBINE SALAD INGREDIENTS AND MIX WITH VINAIGRETTE. REFRIGERATE FOR 1 HOUR. SERVE COLD.

THE LOVELY, merry month of May is finally here. May is a particularly joyful month, for it seems inseparably allied with youth, love, vigor, warmth, and the renewal of life. We feel good in May, as if we're young over again. May is also heavily associated with gardens and garden work, especially in a monastery such as ours, where we're bound to the land, its stewardship, and its cultivation.

Since early April we've been engaged in a steady, disciplined rhythm of spending several hours daily in the solace of our gardens. Early in the season most of the work consisted of removing debris and preparing the garden beds for the planting. With that part of the task complete, our chores entail the planting of seeds and seedlings. Once the planting begins, we won't rest until it's finished sometime in June. Later in the season, when the lettuce and peas are done, we'll engage in a second planting for the forthcoming fall season.

Monks have always taken seriously the biblical admonition that we must eat from the labor of our hands. This means monks must work hard cultivating their vegetable and herb gardens and caring for their orchards. They must always be mindful of the need to produce sufficient food for the monastic table. Since monastic diet according to *The Rule of Saint Benedict* is vegetarian for ascetic reasons, the cultivation of vegetables is vitally important to the daily life of the monastic community.

These days not every monastery is self-sufficient, although most have gardens. We do what we are able to do in our location. For example, at our monastery we don't have an orchard (only a lonely apple tree), partly because our soil is so very rocky but also because our grounds are quite small. Our vegetable and herb gardens, however, are of fairly good size. We have ample space to cultivate all sorts of vegetables, herbs, and crops. Both gardens also include flowering plants since they're such good companions for the rest. I immensely enjoy seeing the lines of zinnias, marigolds, asters, and cosmos interspersed with the rows of vegetables.

As I plant, I think about how intimately the work of the garden is tied to work of the kitchen: Good cuisine depends on fresh produce. For the food to taste good, the ingredients need to be fresh and of the best quality.

Tonight's main dish is a sort of egg timbale that makes good use of the fresh eggs from our chickens. I wouldn't waste my time preparing this dish if I couldn't count on fresh eggs. This concoction, centered around mushrooms and eggs, is accompanied by a simple dish of boiled potatoes garnished with rosemary and garlic and a bowl of fresh green salad. It's a simple but refined meal for an early-spring night.

Food is born out of the lives of those who create it for us, with all of their wisdom, experience and heart.

CAROL MAYBACH

MUSHROOM TIMBALE

18 white mushrooms,
   sliced into small pieces
2 leeks, thinly sliced
   (white parts only)
Salt and pepper
1½ cups heavy cream
½ cup milk
6 eggs
1 teaspoon dried thyme
1 tablespoon butter
4 parsley sprigs or chervil,
   finely chopped

1 Sauté mushrooms and leeks in 1 tablespoon of butter over low-medium heat for 3 to 4 minutes. Stir frequently. Add thyme and continue cooking for 3 or 4 minutes. Remove from heat and set aside.

2 Combine cream and milk in a medium-size casserole and bring it to the boiling point (but do not allow it to boil) over low-medium heat. Remove and set aside.

3 Preheat oven to 350° F. In a deep bowl, beat eggs with a mixer or whisk. Slowly add cream mixture while continuing to mix or whisk.

4 Thoroughly butter 6 or 8 ramekins (small dishes used mostly for crème brûlée). Distribute mushroom-leek mixture evenly among them and pour egg-cream mixture on top.

5 Place each ramekin in a large baking dish filled with water. Do not fill water to more than half the height of the ramekin or the water will spill into the mushroom-leek mixture during baking. Bake at 350° F for 30 to 35 minutes or until timbales are firm. Remove timbales from oven and allow them to cool a bit before you unmold them. They can be served hot or cold, depending on the occasion or season. Unmold them carefully, sprinkle some finely chopped parsley or chervil on top as garnish, and serve.

POTATOES WITH ROSEMARY AND GARLIC

8 SERVINGS

8 good-size potatoes,
   peeled and halved
Pinch of salt
5 tablespoons olive oil
2 sprigs rosemary, needles
   removed and chopped
3 garlic cloves,
   finely chopped
Freshly ground pepper

1 Boil potatoes in salted water for 12 to 15 minutes or until cooked but still firm. Drain and set aside.

2 Heat olive oil in a skillet over low-medium heat. Add chopped rosemary and garlic, stir quickly, and immediately add potatoes. Stir continuously so all sides of the potatoes brown lightly. When potatoes are evenly coated with oil, sprinkle them with freshly ground pepper. Serve immediately as an accompaniment to the timbales.

I</br>N MEDIEVAL TIMES, the month of May was a symbol of the renewal of life and a clear winter defeat. Farmers, landowners, and monks looked forward to a new planting season. Monasteries and parishes carried out the customary processions, which included the blessing of the fields. This was particularly true during what we used to call *Rogation Days*. People of a superstitious nature built enormous bonfires on mountaintops and hillsides and often danced around the flames, imploring the blessings of the "good goddess," the goddess of fertility. A symbol of Mother Earth, she influenced the rhythm of the seasons and the weather to produce an abundant harvest.

No matter what the approach of medieval people, be they Christian or pagan, intercessory prayer and rituals went side by side with planting. Indeed, one had to pray a lot to God for success and blessings on the crops.

Proper monastery gardening is a task *and* an art. It relies on the solid experience and traditions handed down by the monastic gardeners who preceded us. We rely on certain methods and intricate details that are the testament of our past master gardeners. These methods have the advantage of being time-tested, frugal, and thus monastic.

One principle followed over the years at our monastery is that the planting schedule must be synchronized with the rhythms of the liturgy. The seasons of Mother Nature and the seasons of Mother Church blend wonderfully in our daily experience. For example, Lent and Easter—times of spiritual rebirth—happen at the time of year the garden is reborn as well. The stewardship of the monastic land and gardens receives daily inspiration from the celebration of the liturgy. The liturgy, in turn, infuses each season with significance.

Living the mystery of the seasons in full measure helps the monk-gardener become sensitively attuned to the influence of local weather, the proper nurturing of the soil, the knowledge of the right moment for planting and germination, the right time for expanding the cultivation, and the right time to collect the fruits of the harvest. The monastic community and its guests are always grateful to the gardener for the wonderfully fresh vegetables presented at the table.

This evening we present some of these vegetables in a soup. One reason country folk in France, Italy, and Spain seem to always have soup as a first course is that soups are a gentle transition to the main course and the rest of the dinner. A warm soup is always a most desirable appetizer, be it at an elegant dinner or in the informality

Get a garden! What kind you may get matters not, though the soil be light, friable, sandy and hot, or alternatively heavy and rich with stiff clay. Let it lie on a hill, or slope gently away to the level, or sink in an overgrown dell!

WALAFRID STRABO

of home. Monks (and most chefs I know) are quite partial to soups, so I may be accused on occasion of not being completely objective as to their importance.

Rich vegetable soups always seem appropriate and can be made well in advance and kept frozen until they're served. The trick is to give them a smooth finish by adding enough cream to enhance and improve the soup. Just a bit of cream or a well-beaten egg yolk goes a long way to enhance a soup.

Tonight's soup is an exquisite combination of fruits and vegetables that proves once more that fruits have many uses at the table besides dessert.

APPLE, CARROT, LEEK, AND FENNEL SOUP

6 SERVINGS

7 cups vegetable stock or water

1 cup dry white wine

2 Golden Delicious apples, peeled, cored, and chopped

2 carrots, peeled, thinly sliced

2 leeks (white parts only), thinly sliced

3 fresh stalks of fennel, coarsely chopped

1 bay leaf

½ teaspoon dried thyme

Salt and white pepper

½ cup heavy cream

1 small container of low-fat plain yogurt

1 Combine in a good-size soup pot the vegetable stock, wine, apples, carrots, leeks, fennel, bay leaf, thyme, salt, and white pepper. Bring soup to a quick boil, then reduce heat to low-medium. Cover pot and simmer 20 to 25 minutes.

2 Strain soup with a colander, saving liquid part. Remove bay leaf from vegetable mixture. Purée vegetables in a blender or food processor. Add saved liquid and blend well.

3 Reheat soup over medium heat, add cream, and mix well. Ladle soup into soup plates or bowls. Place 1 tablespoon of yogurt in the center of soup as garnish. Serve warm or hot.

TODAY IS sunny with the clouds up high, and a lovely breeze is coming from the south. The apple tree and the lilacs are in full bloom, and their refreshing perfumed air is a tonic of sorts as we go about toiling and planting. Yesterday I planted small seedlings of cabbage, Brussels sprouts, and cauliflower. Today I have several bean varieties to plant, including the Roman pole bean, which always does so well by us and is one of my favorites. Roman pole beans also freeze very well and are a delight to have in winter.

Besides their utilitarian aspect, monastery gardens have always been held in high esteem for spiritual reasons. According to the Scriptures, when God created the world he walked and conversed with Adam and Eve in the Garden of Paradise. Since the fall from grace, we've tried to return to the experience of Paradise by creating gardens all around us.

This idea is especially appealing to monks because it coincides with the very purpose of monastic life, which is to live in communion with God. The early monks built physical enclosures around their gardens, not only to protect them from hungry beasts but primarily to symbolize the sacredness of the space. The garden thus becomes a haven where we can encounter God. The fence built around our own vegetable garden is a constant reminder that it's indeed a special place, a holy ground. Sometimes in the evening, after singing Vespers, I walk and quietly meditate there. The work has stopped, and for a moment I can enjoy the unique presence that fills the entire garden.

One of the enduring qualities of food is that it connects us to hidden memories of our past, to our ancient ancestral roots. How often do you hear these comments in the kitchen: "This is how grandmother prepared this

*Childhood
shows the man
As morning
shows the day.*

JOHN MILTON

dish" or "Aunt Veronique in the Pyrenees made this dessert on birthdays." Food links us to our past and often to concrete persons in that cherished past. Somehow, as we prepare certain dishes, we become children again. We regain our early sense of wonder and innocence. Sometimes the scent alone is enough to evoke ancient memories, cherished souvenirs of our upbringing in our ancestral household and all who inhabited it.

This is particularly true of some homemade desserts. Dessert has a universal appeal. While eating dessert, we become like the little ones we once were. I've seen people in their nineties delighting in ice cream as if they were children, reliving the comfortable, nurturing feelings of youth. The following dessert recipe always registers such sentiments within me.

COCONUT PUDDING
6–8 SERVINGS

6 cups milk
2 cups grated coconut
   (fresh or packaged)
2 cups sugar
1 tablespoon butter
Pinch of salt
¾ cup cornstarch
7 egg yolks, beaten

1 Heat 3 cups of milk in a large saucepan. Add grated coconut, sugar, butter, and salt. Cook over medium heat while stirring continuously. Cook 4 to 5 minutes or until sugar and coconut are well blended.

2 In a separate saucepan, mix 3 cups milk and cornstarch. (You needn't heat it at this point.) Stir cornstarch until it dissolves in milk (be sure there are no lumps left). Whisk in eggs and mix until well blended.

3 Add egg mixture to coconut mixture and cook over low–medium heat, stirring constantly 15 to 20 minutes or until custard thickens. Avoid bringing custard to a boil.

4 Rinse a 1½-quart baking dish with cold water. Pour hot custard into wet dish. Allow it to cool. Place dish under broiler for a few minutes or until custard turns brown on top.

5 Cover custard with aluminum foil and refrigerate for a few hours. Serve cold.

Ascension

AFTER A MUCH-NEEDED RAIN over the past two days, I welcomed dawn with joy. The early light was unspoiled, perfectly apt for the Feast of the Ascension, which we celebrate today. Today we can be confirmed and strengthened by the knowledge that Christ, our Savior, has reached the end of his earthly pilgrimage. He waits now with open arms for us to join him: "In my Father's house there are many dwelling-places. If it were not so, would I have told you that I go to prepare a place for you?" (John 14:2).

Our first garden was planted in 1978, the year our small monastery was established here in New York's Hudson Valley. We had hard times at the beginning—the soil is little more than stones, and the garden was too far from our buildings. Our property is hilly and covered with woods, and the garden was easily accessible to deer, raccoons, and other animals. We were overly ambitious and made a garden too large for our needs.

After a poor first harvest, we moved the garden closer to the monastery building next to the sheep barn. This discouraged the deer, made it easier to get sheep manure to the garden, and gave the garden protection from heavy winds.

Our garden is 100 percent organic. We maintain its fertility with manure from our sheep and chickens and with the compost we build each year. Fertilizing the garden is a never-ending task because of the poor, rocky soil.

Our first root crops were small and misshapen because they couldn't grow deep enough. In the early days, we didn't even try to grow potatoes. But with tenacity and patience, we've made notable improvements in the soil, including removing as many rocks as possible. We used many of these rocks to build our chapel.

The garden is divided into two equal sections. One side has long, raised beds where we cultivate salad and root vegetables, spinach, sorrel, peas, leeks, onions, shallots, flowers, and some herbs. In the other half, we grow on level ground larger vegetable plants that require more space: squash, pumpkins, cucumbers, tomatoes, eggplants, peppers, poll beans, string beans, Swiss chard, cabbages, broccoli, Brussels sprouts, and cauliflower as well as a variety of potatoes.

In the center of the garden stands a statue of Saint Fiacre, a monk and the patron saint of gardeners. The statue is surrounded by pots of flowers. His protection over the gardens is beseeched daily. Two small patches built into equal squares, one in front of the statue and the other in the back, are devoted to the cultivation of herbs: basil, parsley, thyme, oregano, cilantro, sage, dill, rosemary, and garlic. We

In my Father's house there are many dwelling-places.

JOHN 14:2

use another herb garden for drying and ornamentation, but the one in the vegetable garden is exclusively for fresh kitchen use.

It's almost two months since I planted the first peas on March 25, the Feast of the Annunciation. Peas are usually the first things I plant in the garden, two weeks earlier than lettuce and radishes. It's no surprise, then, that we have an early harvest of this storied springtime vegetable and delight in its incredible pleasures. From mid May to mid June the peas are abundant, and I greatly enjoy preparing a fresh green soup for the evening meal. It's usually delicious, nurturing, and wonderfully nourishing. When I find morel mushrooms in our woods, I often combine them with the peas to achieve a soup rich in flavor and gentle in texture.

We planted the first peas on the Feast of the Annunciation, so it's appropriate that we harvest and consume them on this glorious feast of the Ascension of the Lord, when the earthly days of Jesus came to an end and he ascended to the Father.

MONASTERY SPRING-PEA SOUP

4–6 SERVINGS

3 tablespoons butter or
    regular olive oil
2 leeks (white parts only),
    thinly sliced
1 celery stalk, thinly sliced
½ pound morel or plain white
    mushrooms, cleaned and
    thinly sliced
6 cups vegetable stock or water
3 cups shelled fresh peas
Salt and freshly ground pepper
2 egg yolks, beaten
½ cup heavy cream
Fresh chervil or parsley,
    finely chopped

1 In a large soup pot, melt butter over low-medium heat. Add leeks and celery. Stir continuously for 3 to 4 minutes. Add mushrooms and stir 1 to 2 minutes. Add stock or water, peas, and salt and pepper to taste. Raise heat to medium, cover pot, and bring to a boil.

2 Reduce heat to low-medium and let simmer 25 to 30 minutes or until peas are tender. Remove from heat and let cool. Set aside.

3 Slowly purée soup in a blender in small batches. To the last batch, add beaten eggs and cream. Blend thoroughly.

4 Reheat soup in the pot and blend all ingredients well. Serve soup warm and top with finely chopped chervil or parsley.

Sorrel is one of the first greens to appear in our garden during early spring, and I try to incorporate it into the season's recipes. It has a particular sour flavor and is one of the more popular vegetables throughout France. It is often used in simple home and monastic kitchens as well as by the chefs of the haute cuisine française. *Again, this delicious vegetable can be prepared in endless ways. This recipe is rather simple and basic and would please most people.*

ASCENSION DAY SORREL AU GRATIN

4 SERVINGS

2 cups water
8 cups thinly cut sorrel (or spinach)
3–4 tablespoons olive oil
1 medium-size onion, thinly sliced
1 cup béchamel sauce
   (recipe follows)
2 egg yolks, beaten
⅓ cup grated cheese

BÉCHAMEL SAUCE
2 tablespoons butter or margarine
2 tablespoons cornstarch or flour
2 cups milk
1 tablespoon dry sherry (optional)
Salt and pepper
Pinch of nutmeg (optional)

1 In a large stainless-steel saucepan, bring water to a boil. Add sorrel and let it boil for no more than 3 minutes. Drain thoroughly.

2 Pour oil into skillet and sauté sliced onion over medium heat for about 2 minutes or until it begins to turn golden. Preheat oven to 350° F.

3 Prepare béchamel sauce by melting the butter in a good-size stainless-steel pan over medium-low heat. While stirring continuously with a whisk, add cornstarch, milk little by little, sherry, salt, pepper, and nutmeg. Continue stirring. When sauce begins to boil, reduce heat and continue cooking slowly until it thickens. This sauce is excellent with fish and vegetables and is a necessary base for soufflés, omelettes, and other egg dishes.

4 Beat egg yolks and add to béchamel sauce. Blend thoroughly, then add the well-drained sorrel and onion and blend mixture very well.

5 Pour mixture into a well-buttered flat baking dish and sprinkle grated cheese over the entire surface. Bake at 350° F for about 15 minutes. The gratin is ready when it takes on an even, thick consistency. Serve hot.

Clafoutis is a traditional dessert said to have originated in the central part of France, yet it's so well known and popular throughout France that each region has its own version. Though traditionally made with cherries, any in-season fruit can be substituted.

PEAR CLAFOUTIS

6–8 SERVINGS

4 pears
1 cup milk
3 eggs
½ cup white granulated sugar
2 tablespoons cognac or vanilla
Confectioners' (powdered) sugar

1 Preheat oven to 350° F.

2 Peel and slice pears.

3 Prepare batter: Place milk, eggs, white granulated sugar, and cognac in blender and whirl thoroughly at high speed for 1 or 2 minutes.

4 Generously butter a square baking dish about 1 to 2 inches deep. Pour about ¼ of the batter into the baking dish and place in oven for about 2 minutes or until batter has set. Remove from oven and arrange sliced pears evenly on top. Sprinkle a bit of confectioners' (powdered) sugar over the fruit. Pour remaining batter over fruit, smoothing evenly. Place in center of oven and bake for about 40 minutes. Clafoutis is done when the top puffs and turns brown, though still remaining custardlike. Remove from oven, sprinkle confectioners' (powdered) sugar on top, and serve while clafoutis is still warm.

Pentecost

THE FEAST of the Pentecost usually arrives in late May or early June, times of almost perpetually perfect weather. Today is no different. The countryside is transformed by the resurgent, magical light of spring. It bodes well for Pentecost, a time of plenitude and fullness. Today we complete the days of the Easter cycle, exactly fifty days after the resurrection of Jesus, and experience the descent of the Holy Spirit into our lives. He comes to reveal to each of us the meaning of all Jesus taught during his years on earth: "I have said these things to you while I am still with you. But the Advocate, the Holy Spirit, whom the Father will send in my name, will teach you everything, and remind you of all that I have said to you" (Jn 14: 25-26).

As we approach the end of May, we begin to leave the foods of winter behind. Suddenly, the new, tender salad greens planted but a few weeks ago begin to appear in our gardens, and we awaken to the surprise of new delights for our table. Fresh flavors and textures find a place in our dishes, especially in our salads, creating a sort of magic and endless comfort to our palates.

A mixed-green salad is very basic, but when tossed with a variety of crunchy garden greens, smoothed with a fruity olive oil, and tempered by an astringently flavored vinegar, it turns into an irresistible dish. The dressing or vinaigrette can be prepared in a blender; however, I much prefer to prepare it the old-fashioned way, by pouring the right amount of ingredients over the salad at the last minute and then tossing it all together with my own hands. The end result is an appetizing dish that nurtures both body and soul.

Salads are part of the daily fare of ordinary French homes. They may not always contain such a variety of greens, but whatever they're made of, they never cease to appeal to any palate, especially after a good main course.

PENTECOST SALAD
6–8 SERVINGS

1 head Boston lettuce
1 head Bibb or leaf lettuce
1 bunch arugula
1 bunch fresh baby spinach leaves
1 bunch watercress
Chopped chives and chervil

VINAIGRETTE
1 teaspoon salt
½ teaspoon freshly ground pepper
2 tablespoons wine vinegar
6 tablespoons olive oil

1 Wash greens thoroughly and separate individual leaves. Do not cut or split leaves, only stems. Drain leaves completely, roll them with paper towels, and refrigerate until ready to serve so they stay fresh and crisp.

2 Just before serving, mix greens in a salad bowl.

3 Prepare a simple vinaigrette: place salt and pepper in a cup or bowl. Add vinegar and stir thoroughly. Add oil and stir until ingredients are completely blended.

4 Pour the vinaigrette over greens and toss lightly. Sprinkle with finely chopped chives and/or chervil.

JUNE

*T*WOKE UP early this morning to gain time for prayer and reading. There was a stillness in the air, a haziness I've learned to associate with late spring. I love these intimate moments in early morning when the only sounds are birds singing and sheep bleating. These early hours are ideal for prayer. Occasionally, after singing the morning Office, I usually take the Bible and comfortably engage in what is monastically called *lectio divina*. I particularly enjoy doing my period of *lectio* outdoors. Scripture and nature complement each other well. Through both, God speaks to us daily. Quietly and eloquently, he reveals himself in sacred Scripture and in his creations which are, after all, his handiwork.

Reading, studying, and praying over Scripture are important components of the monastic day. I read, study, sing, and often pray over Scripture in solitude, but this solitude is always in communion with the one, whole Church established by the Lord. Attachment and reverence to sacred Scripture is therefore attachment and reverence to Christ Himself.

This morning, as I plunged into the reading and meditation of Scripture, I chose Saint Paul's second letter to the Thessalonians. Although I've read this letter often, this time his specific approach to food stirred me. The apostle connects the "right" to eat with the "obligation" to labor and work. He tells the Thessalonians, "For even when we were with you, we gave you this command: Anyone unwilling to work should not eat" (3:10).

Later, Saint Paul insists to those early Christians not only the necessity of work, but also the manner of how to work and behave in the workplace: "Now such persons we command and exhort in the Lord Jesus Christ to do their work quietly and to earn their own living" (3:12). Saint Benedict would totally agree with Saint Paul as to the manner in which monks must work in the monastery: quietly, silently, and busy with their hands—their minds free, their hearts set on God alone. Laboring this way daily is also a more effective and productive way of contributing to the economy of the monastery. Centuries of monastic tradition attest to that.

The afternoon hours are dedicated to garden work. Helped by today's insights from Saint Paul, I remind myself that this humble, menial routine is full of dignity and grace. Jesus, the humble carpenter from Nazareth, worked daily at his trade, as did his foster father, the honorable Saint Joseph.

Today my first task in the garden is to continue weeding the radish and salad patch. Every year I plant a variety of radishes and salad greens early so we can start

In our hearts is the heavenly fire of grace. If we pray and meditate on the love of Christ, we add wood to the fire and our hearts burn with longing for God.

PSEUDO-MACARIUS

picking them for our daily salads in late May and early June. As I weed, I pick good-size radishes and start planning our early dinner.

One of the joys of cooking and eating seasonally grown produce is that feeling of freshness, of newness, of crunchiness—that mood of spontaneity this gorgeous early produce inspires. We feel like children all over again. I remember coming home from school to wonderful crunchy radish sandwiches prepared with fresh bread and the first radishes of the season. They're a delicious, quick way to enhance a simple monastic dinner. A warm soup and a good, hearty sandwich made of fresh radishes and some greens is all I need for a simple weekday monastic meal when there isn't time for lengthy cooking.

To start, I wash the radishes thoroughly and place them in a bowl filled with ice to keep them fresh until the time comes to use them. We're blessed to have these great radishes right now in season in our own garden. Those who don't cultivate their own gardens can find locally grown radishes at any farmers' market.

SLICED-RADISH SANDWICH, FRENCH STYLE

4 SERVINGS

1 fresh French baguette
  (long French bread)
Salted butter
1 large bunch of fresh radishes,
  trimmed, washed,
  and thinly sliced

OPTIONAL: 1 LONG CUCUMBER, PEELED AND THINLY SLICED

1 A few fresh watercress sprigs, trimmed

2 Cut baguette lengthwise into four equal slices.

3 Generously butter each slice.

4 Arrange and evenly distribute radish slices on bread, covering entire surface. Add a line of freshly sliced cucumber (optional). Add watercress over the cucumbers. Top with corresponding bread slice. Press firmly once.

5 Place sandwiches in a large serving plate or platter. Cover with a clean towel and let stand for at least 45 minutes before eating. Enjoy them after a bowl of warm, hearty soup.

NOTHING is so beautiful as a clear, sunny day in June. From the top of the hillside, I looked around this morning in all directions and saw nothing but the surrounding countryside enveloped in rare, quiet beauty.

As the years go by, I love more and more the enchanting beauty of this corner of the world. God manifests himself in the minutiae of daily life—in the changing of the weather and the seasons, in the unexpected visitor who occasionally arrives at our doors, in the calmness of the monastic enclosure, in the simplicity and smell of our farm animals, in the harmony and intimacy of our gardens, and in the glorious trees that shade us in these early summer days. For this, I can only utter with our Holy Father Saint Benedict, "May God be glorified in all things."

The beauty of our land and the harmony around me are great incentives to continue toiling daily. Some days I'm exhausted. Then I look around and see how God has toiled to uphold his creation and sustain its beauty. I get up once more, take the shovel, and continue weeding. Then I water the garden beds that need it most. There will be time for rest later, I tell myself. For now, it's time to labor and cooperate with the Author of all creation.

Thinking like this every day lightens the burden. I often pause to reflect on how we are all called to be stewards of this magnificent Earth he has entrusted to us and how this work must continue steadfastly, faithfully, and gently in this spot he has assigned us.

I often use the psalms or poetry for inspiration and extra encouragement as I go about my daily work. The Jesus Prayer helps me keep my balance, and the inspiration that comes from spiritual poets is a great incentive to look beyond the daily trivia. We all need that sort of push, that bit of inspiration as we plunge into the vicissitudes of our daily routines. It makes the tasks easier, smoother. The same thing happens while toiling in the kitchen, but there I have the occasional luxury of listening to Bach and other composers. Music, poetry, and prayer combine to build harmony while plowing through the task at hand. More important, they help bring inner harmony into our lives.

Our monastery kitchen gives ample opportunity for cultivating this sort of harmony. In one corner rests the wood-burning stove and hearth, the focus of the room during our long winters. Above the stove hangs a large icon of Christ the Lord, an early reproduction from the catacombs. This icon keeps us centered on the Presence that really matters.

The ambience of quiet conviviality in this kitchen inspires prayer and work. Both tasks go hand in hand in a monastery, for under no circumstances must we forget our Lord's reminder to Martha while laboring in her busy kitchen: "There is need of only one thing" (Luke 10:42).

The "road" does not belong to you nor is it presently under your control. But as you walk, and step succeeds step, enjoy each moment as it comes and then continue on your "way."

SAINT BASIL THE GREAT

Tonight in our modest refectory we will enjoy one of the blessings of the spring season: asparagus. Just this morning a local grower brought us a fresh bunch we can delight in for days. The first thing that came to my mind was to make asparagus soup from scratch. But the more I thought about it, the more I was led to prepare it with pasta as the main course. In this monastery kitchen, asparagus is treated with utmost respect and given the preference and attention it deserves.

In late May and June, when asparagus is tender and fresh with maximum flavor, color, and texture that please any palate, is the best time to treat ourselves to asparagus dishes. Tomorrow or the day after I will rejoice in preparing asparagus timbale, which I make only when asparagus is in season. I love to make it with the white asparagus we eat in France, but white asparagus isn't as common here and the ones in the supermarket are frightfully expensive for a simple monastery like ours.

The recipe here is made without meat; you can add strips of ham or prosciutto, but the cheeses contain enough protein that meat isn't necessary.

Since the asparagus is fresh, it needn't be peeled. Simply wash and trim each spear at the bottom before cooking. Discard the bottom.

FUSILLI PASTA WITH FRESH ASPARAGUS 4–6 SERVINGS

1½ pounds fresh, tender asparagus, trimmed and cut into 2-inch segments
5 tablespoons virgin olive oil
1 pound fusilli pasta
½ cup mascarpone or ricotta cheese
½ cup grated Parmesan cheese
Freshly ground pepper
½ cup hazelnuts, roasted and coarsely chopped
⅓ cup fresh chervil, finely chopped
Grated Parmesan cheese

1 Boil asparagus in salted water a maximum of 5 minutes. It must remain tender but firm (al dente). Drain and set aside at room temperature.

2 Pour olive oil into a large pot of boiling water, add salt, and cook pasta until it's al dente. Stir from time to time. Drain pasta and save 1 cup of the cooking water.

3 Return pasta to the pot. Add mascarpone or ricotta cheese, grated Parmesan cheese, asparagus, and pepper. Stir well over low-medium heat. If necessary, gradually add about ⅓ of the saved pasta water.

4 Empty pasta mixture into a large serving bowl. Top with roasted hazelnuts, chervil, and grated Parmesan cheese. Serve immediately.

*J*UNE is all about a basket of strawberries, a friend recently said to me. With that in mind, after a quick lunch I place several empty baskets in the back of the car and drive north in search of strawberries. The farm I go to has an early harvest because they protect their crops from late frosts with heavy plastic. Invariably, by mid June their strawberries begin to arrive, and so do their customers.

There's something special about strawberries over all other types of fruits or berries. Strawberries are beautifully scented—almost sensual—tender, delicious, and always agreeable to the palate. It's one of the most popular fruits, especially the small extra-sweet type called in France *fraise de bois,* which often grow wild in our gardens. The strawberry is the first fruit of the season; it arrives early and promptly, announcing the arrival of the beautiful days of summer. The strawberry, called *fragaria* in Latin because of its perfume and exquisite fragrance, is extremely rich in vitamin C, among other nutrients. It also contains the fiber we need for proper digestion.

One reason I prefer fresh strawberries from a farm to supermarket strawberries is that this farm cultivates them organically. Also, I can pick my own strawberries, choosing the best in the size that I prefer. I'm not fond of the large strawberries we often see in the supermarkets. They seem more full of water than anything else. I prefer smaller or medium-size, firm and fully red. When picked gently, correctly, and refrigerated promptly, these strawberries stay fresh for several days.

To serve them, simply take them out of the refrigerator thirty minutes before the meal. It's that simple. Fresh strawberries can be served with vanilla ice cream, plain yogurt, sugar and a bit of fresh lemon juice, or sugar mixed with Cointreau, sherry (Jerez or other), or any of your favorite liqueurs, alone or topped with a freshly made Crème Chantilly.

Tonight I'll prepare them the old-fashioned and most common way of serving them in France, with sugar and plain red wine. It's quick, simple, and always flavorful.

What a wealth of
beauty do I glean.
When June time
takes me wondering!
Thomas Curtis Clark
and what is so rare
as a day in June?
Then, if ever,
come perfect days.
Whether we look or
whether we listen,
We hear life murmur,
or see it glisten.

JAMES R. LOWELL

STRAWBERRIES IN WINE

4–6 SERVINGS

1 pound fresh strawberries
2 cups good-quality red wine
1 cup refined white sugar
5 whole cloves
1 zest of orange peel,
  lightly pounded

1 Wash and clean strawberries. Trim the tops. Gently halve strawberries lengthwise. Set aside or refrigerate.

2 Pour wine into a good-size saucepan and add sugar, cloves, and orange zest. Boil for 5 minutes while stirring steadily. Turn off heat, remove cloves and orange peel, and let wine mixture rest 15 to 20 minutes. Refrigerate until ready to serve.

3 Place strawberries in a serving bowl, pour wine mixture over the fruit. Toss lightly and serve immediately. This dessert must always be served cool.

BASIC STRAWBERRY JAM

4 HALF PINTS

1 pound fresh strawberries
1 pound sugar
Juice of 2 lemons
2 tablespoons strawberry
  or similar liqueur
1 packet organic
  liquid pectin

1 Wash, dry, and hull strawberries. Place them in a large, heavy, nonreactive pot. Add sugar, lemon juice, and strawberry liqueur. Stir to coat strawberries, crushing them slightly.

2 Cook mixture over medium heat, stirring constantly, until it comes to a rolling boil. Add pectin and boil for 1 more minute, still stirring constantly.

3 Remove pot from heat and skim off foam. Ladle quickly into sterilized, warm jars. Cap according to manufacturer's directions and process 10 minutes in hot-water bath.

HOW TO explain the enchantment we all feel during these early summer days? Neighbors and friends begin planning summer outings, picnics, vacations where they can enjoy the glories of open space, trips to organic farms or farmers' markets, and the delights of outdoor grilling and dining with cherished friends and family. Summer has so much to offer, and when well planned by its aficionados, it usually delivers.

The hazy, lazy days of summer, with their tantalizing invitation to outdoor living, free us from the oppressive custom of restricting our meals to the indoors. Indoor eating is fine most of the year, but once the heat arrives we need a break. We go beyond the mere conventionality of indoor meals and freely embrace cooking, grilling, and eating in the open air as much and as often as we can.

The simple dishes prepared for these informal outdoor meals reflect the character, freshness, fruitfulness, and creativity the season inspires. They speak of the glories and joviality of summer living, of the abundance of the garden, and of God's blessings on the season. Welcome summer, we say, with a sort of cooking that corresponds to it.

This first outdoor meal of the season will start with a lovely and tender mesclun salad mixed with red onions and roasted peppers. The mesclun took a bit longer to arrive this year, but it's finally here and now is the ideal time to enjoy it. A few things warm and brighten my heart as much as these delicious, tender little salad greens whose seeds I faithfully bring back every year from the south of France.

The rest of the menu, a blend of quick and informal dishes such as the lentil salad, is readily designed for a simple outdoor meal. These recipes make our friends feel at home on our simple porch, which overlooks the barn where our sheep quietly say goodnight to the day.

CHUNKY AVOCADO SALAD
6–8 SERVINGS

4 firm avocados, peeled and diced into large chunks
3 tablespoons lemon juice
1 medium red onion, minced
10 medium-size fresh radishes, washed and halved
1 green bell pepper, diced
10 black pitted olives, halved
8 fresh cilantro sprigs, finely chopped
Extra-virgin olive oil
Salt and freshly ground pepper

1 Place avocado dices in a large salad bowl. Pour lemon juice and toss gently.

2 Add minced onion, radishes, pepper, olives, and cilantro. Toss and mix ingredients.

3 Add olive oil, salt, and pepper. Toss gently until ingredients are equally coated. Serve immediately with tortilla chips.

MESCLUN SALAD WITH PEPPERS AND MOZZARELLA CHEESE

6–8 SERVINGS

2 medium-size red peppers,
  halved lengthwise and seeded
2 medium-size yellow peppers,
  halved lengthwise and seeded
4 tablespoons regular olive oil
1 medium-size red onion, peeled
  and sliced in half-moons
5 ounces fresh mozzarella, diced
1½ cup fresh mesclun,
  washed and cleaned
4 tablespoons extra-virgin olive oil
2 teaspoons red-wine vinegar
Sea salt and freshly ground pepper

1 Preheat oven to 400° F. Place pepper tops on a large-rimmed, flat baking dish. Sprinkle olive oil over them. Roast peppers for 25 to 30 minutes or until they turn brown. Remove peppers from oven and allow them to cool for about 10 minutes. Peel them and slice them into strips lengthwise. Place them in a large salad bowl.

2 Add onion and mozzarella cheese to the bowl.

3 Add fresh mesclun to bowl. Sprinkle with remaining olive oil, red-wine vinegar. Add salt and pepper to taste. Toss gently and serve.

LENTILS WITH PARSLEY AND MINT

6–8 SERVINGS

1½ cup lentils (preferably
  the small, crunchy type)
Water
1 red onion, medium-size, minced
8 sprigs of flat-leafed parsley,
  chopped
1 cup fresh mint, chopped
1 bunch scallions, finely chopped
1 small English cucumber, diced
  (peeled if not from your garden)
2 cups cherry tomatoes, washed
  and dried
⅓ cup fresh lemon juice
¼ cup virgin olive oil
Sea salt and freshly ground pepper

1 Combine lentils and water in a good-size casserole and bring to a boil. Cook for about 20 minutes or until lentils are tender but still whole and crunchy. Drain them thoroughly and place in a large salad bowl.

2 Add minced onion, chopped parsley, mint, scallions, cucumber, and cherry tomatoes (whole or halved). Toss gently and refrigerate until ready to serve.

3 Just before serving, mix in a bowl or measuring cup the lemon juice, olive oil, salt, and vinegar. Mix well. Pour over salad and toss once more until elements are equally coated. Serve chilled.

WHEN I CONCEIVED THE IDEA for this book, all I wanted to do was share the intimate moments of a monastery kitchen and convey the spirituality that inspires our daily cooking. In a monastery, the food we grow in the garden and later consume at the table connects us in a unique way. This is really what I enjoy describing in these pages.

Growing and cultivating our own food is something monks do our entire lives; eating and enjoying the fruit of our labors is the humble reward. Food is such a primal reality in everyone's life, in or out of the monastery. Food connects us—it's the great equalizer. Jesus was never more human than when he sat at a table and shared the unique joy of eating a good meal with his friends or disciples. In doing that, he taught us the value he assigned to food and its intimate sharing among friends.

But he didn't stop there. He went a step further and incorporated the greatest gift he left us in the form of food. He deliberately left us his own body in the form of bread as sustenance and nourishment for our souls and bodies; he left us his own blood in the form of drink. Thus, he reminded us that the whole meaning of the Incarnation comes down to this: He is one of us, someone who eats and drinks daily and finds joy in the appreciation of it. The Son of Man came eating and drinking.

Today the Catholic Church calendar marks the Solemnity of Saint John the Baptist, a desert ascetic and thus a prototype and model for all those in monastic life. He was particularly close to Jesus, related to him.

Today, as I ponder the theme of food in Jesus' teachings and actions while also observing his great tribute to John the Baptist, I can't help but see a contrast between the Master and his most loyal admirer and disciple. Jesus, though he lived and observed a life of great simplicity, doesn't appear to be as austere and ascetic as John the Baptizer. Jesus rejoiced in the jovial company of his friends and disciples and enjoyed the meals they shared. He used the setting of a meal to keep company and to reveal himself to certain disciples on the way to Emmaus. In contrast, John the Baptist often fasted and lived mostly on locusts and honey.

Are these differences irreconcilable for Christians, or can we learn from both Jesus the Master and John the disciple? As with many other Gospel predicaments, where certain teachings seem opposite, we can discover that these practices are complementary and can have equal bearing on our lives as the Master's disciples. Jesus' demonstration of his appreciation and enjoyment of food was a clear acknowledgment of the goodness of God for all his children. Food, therefore, when used

The crown of a good disposition is humility.

ARABIAN PROVERB

94

and enjoyed in proper moderation, can be one more means of rediscovering and acknowledging God's presence.

The example and teachings of John the Baptist remind us of equally important teachings of Jesus. Yes, Jesus loved and enjoyed food and the good company of his disciples, but he also fasted and practiced solitude in the desert. He reminded us there is a time and place for fasting, just as there is for feasting. He strongly rejected the sort of fast performed publicly to receive the admiration of others. Jesus' disciples were encouraged to pray and fast in secret, where only the heavenly Father would be aware of their actions.

Tonight's dinner incorporates a delicious dish that originated in my cherished region of the Pyrenees. I carry the thought and memory of those beloved mountains in my heart—sometimes I ache for them—so it's not surprising that often in cooking I find my inspiration in the cuisine of that region. Tonight we will eat eggplant cooked with plenty of garlic. It's usually accompanied by a salad of locally grown greens, which helps with digestion. Any simple green salad will serve that purpose.

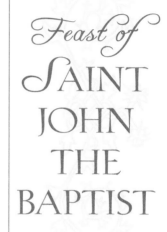

Feast of
SAINT JOHN THE BAPTIST

EGGPLANT WITH GARLIC

6–8 SERVINGS

6 large garlic cloves, peeled and
　　halved lengthwise
½ cup extra-virgin olive oil
½ teaspoon sea salt
¼ teaspoon freshly ground pepper
3 tablespoons dried thyme, rosemary,
　　bay leaf, and oregano, crumbled
8 small Japanese-style eggplants,
　　halved lengthwise
4 garlic cloves, minced and
　　finely chopped
Freshly grated cheese

1 Preheat oven to 350° F.

2 Place garlic cloves in a deep bowl and pour olive oil over them. Let rest for ½ hour. Remove cloves and slice them into thin lengthwise slivers. Mix remaining oil with salt, pepper, and dry herbs.

3 Place eggplant halves in a well-buttered ovenproof dish. Make 5 or 6 holes or indentations in each eggplant half at varying distances from each other. Slip a garlic sliver in each hole. Brush eggplant tops with seasoned-herbed oil. Top with garlic. Wrap entire dish in aluminum foil and place in oven. Bake 25 to 30 minutes.

4 Remove dish from oven. Sprinkle with grated cheese. Serve with a fresh green salad.

Time is too slow

for those who wait,

too swift for

those who fear,

too long for

those who grieve,

too short for

those who rejoice;

but for those

who love,

time is eternity.

HENRY VAN DYKE

*S*UMMER PRESENTS EXCITING IDEAS to everyone who loves to cook, from master chefs to ordinary cooks. Fresh ingredients from local gardens and farmers' markets are available almost everywhere. The fresh and flavorful ingredients found at road stands or local fresh-produce markets can inspire even beginner cooks, so dinner needn't always be a repetition of last night's leftovers.

The secret of a simple and good meal is to plan. I plan the main course first and then the accompaniments, for example, a cold soup that can be made the day before and chilled or a robust or delicate salad of meat, fish, or eggs to follow or accompany the main course.

On summer days when one doesn't wish to prolong cooking over a hot stove, a dish of plain greens in the form of a salad can become the best accompaniment to a dish of roasted beef, ham, chicken, or fish. On weekdays fresh fruit, ice cream, or sorbet complete a homemade meal in good and honest fashion. After such a meal, there's still time to enjoy a healthy walk around the block, deeply breathing the fresh summer air and enjoying the clear starry skies, truly gifts of the season.

This month I harvested peas, and now the first tender turnips are beginning to arrive. I love both peas and young turnips, especially the variety I bring from France, which is a bit smaller than the common turnip here in the States. This particular turnip seems to have a bit more taste; it takes about forty-five days to mature, so when it's planted early it can be harvested in early summer.

The peas and the arrival of the turnips inspire tonight's supper. A simple risotto encompasses both ingredients. A crisp, green salad of home or locally grown greens in a piquant honey vinaigrette served with flavorful local artisanal cheese complements the main course.

The pleasingly simple seasonal recipe described here illustrates how one can best profit during the summer months from what is available locally, save time in the kitchen during weekdays, and yet unfailingly serve something that can be enjoyed by everyone, especially vegetarians.

This type of inventive summer cooking reflects loving attention to detail and to what is grown in the garden or the immediate vicinity. It consists of food prepared with much love and gusto. And love, as we know, comes from God. Love spices food like no other ingredient. Love is a foretaste of the new creation granted to us in Christ; as such, it sanctifies our meal preparation as much as it makes us apprehend more fully the reality of God's gifts and blessings in the food we consume.

RISOTTO WITH PEAS AND TURNIPS

5 tablespoons virgin olive oil
1 medium-size onion, chopped
1 garlic clove, minced
2 young turnips, trimmed and diced
½ cup green peas, shelled
1 cup arborio rice
Dash of fresh or dried thyme
4 cups boiling vegetable broth
   (or chicken for nonvegetarians)
   or water
Salt and freshly ground pepper
   Freshly grated Parmesan cheese

1 Pour olive oil into a heavy saucepan, add onion and garlic and sauté for about 1 minute over low-moderate heat. Stir frequently. Add turnips, peas, rice, and thyme. Continue sautéing and stirring for about 2 minutes or until all rice is evenly coated.

2 Add 2 cups of the boiling broth or water, raise the heat to medium, and continue stirring until almost all liquid is absorbed. Add the remaining broth or water and stir constantly until all liquid is absorbed and rice is cooked and tender. Turn off heat, cover, and let stand 1 or 2 minutes before serving. Sprinkle with freshly grated Parmesan cheese and serve hot.

When the summer squash arrive in the garden in late June or early July, I immediately start using them in our daily cooking. They're very practical because they don't take long to cook or grill, and they're delicious when young and tender. This simple recipe well accompanies whatever meat, fish or egg dish will be served for the main course.

SUMMER SQUASH JULIENNE

1 onion, thinly sliced
6 tablespoons olive oil
2 medium-size young tender zucchini,
   cut into long thin strips)
2 medium-size young tender yellow squash,
   cut into long thin strips
1 medium-size red pepper, cut into long
   thin strips
Salt and freshly ground pepper
Freshly chopped chervil

1 Cook onions in olive oil over low-medium heat in a large nonstick skillet or saucepan. Stir frequently.

2 Add zucchini, yellow squash, red pepper, salt, and pepper and continue stirring until vegetables are cooked and tender. Sprinkle with chopped chervil. Mix well and serve immediately.

ASPARAGUS, NEW POTATOES, AND HARD-BOILED EGGS WITH VINAIGRETTE

6 SERVINGS

6 medium-size new potatoes, peeled and left whole

6 eggs, hard-boiled, peeled, and halved lengthwise

2 pounds fresh asparagus, trimmed

VINAIGRETTE

1 shallot, minced

½ cup extra-virgin olive oil

4 tablespoons red-wine vinegar

1 tablespoon French mustard, Dijon or other

1 teaspoon sugar

Salt and freshly ground pepper

1 Boil potatoes in salted water until cooked and tender. Drain and set aside.

2 Cook and peel eggs. Halve lengthwise and set aside.

3 Prepare vinaigrette by thoroughly whisking the shallot, olive oil, red-wine vinegar, mustard, sugar, salt, and pepper. Set aside.

4 Cook asparagus spears in salted water for about 5 minutes or until they're crisp and tender. Rinse with cold water and drain.

5 Arrange on each serving plate equal portions of asparagus, one whole potato, and 2 hard-boiled egg halves. Drizzle evenly with vinaigrette. Serve at room temperature. This dish is a complete meal in itself—a perfect light dish for a summer night.

JULY

WHEN JULY ARRIVES, a sigh of relief fills the countryside. Even the very name of the month sounds like a sweet melody that contains the promise of summer's many secret delights. Summer is a time of relaxation, magic, and jubilation. Summer offers endless possibilities, particularly for people immersed in their gardens and daily kitchen chores.

I've been closely watching the rapid changes taking place in the landscape. The ground has become hot and dry, so we must water the garden often. The surrounding hills are hazy, almost crying for the blessings of a rain. There is no breath in the wind, yet I sense a sweet fragrance in our garden.

In July, everything seems to grow intensely, richly, fruitfully. As I take my early daily walk inspecting the gardens, I pause. I enjoy being attentive to the now, sensitive to the present moment. Becoming aware of the gift of the here and now is a contemplative practice as well as an art form. As I continue my walk and inspections, I notice our vegetables are ripening rapidly. Soon, very soon, we'll be harvesting the rewards of our labors.

Our seasonal monastic work concentrates on garden chores. The heat and I are not very good companions, so during these very warm days I resort to preparing mostly salad dishes that limit my interaction with a hot stove. I enjoy salad-making. Like soups, salads offer many possibilities for the cook. Over the years I've learned to categorize salads in many ways, including by origin, serving occasion, and length of preparation. Any astute cook can find joy and a sense of fulfillment in the ingenious preparation of a good salad.

There are many cooked dishes for which I think the perfect accompaniment is simply a well-made salad, rather than cooked vegetables: the fresh flavor and crisp texture provide a pleasant contrast.

ROSE ELLIOT

Salad-making is universal. One finds salad dishes in every culture and on every continent. Some international salads have become classic recipes because they've been around for centuries. Take, for instance, *salade niçoise,* caesar salad, mimosa salad, and Waldorf salad. Each is found on menus across the world, from the fanciest five-star restaurants to the humblest bistros. Our fondness for these classic international salads has increased over the past few decades due in part to the amount of international traveling done by Americans who discover the treasures of local cuisine.

The salad for today's dinner allows us to revisit distant places such as England through the use of its famous Stilton cheese and allows us to evoke in the intimacy of our kitchens memories of delightful flavors once tasted in a faraway place. It's an excellent salad to serve after a main course.

BABY SPINACH, WATERCRESS, AND STILTON CHEESE SALAD
6 SERVINGS

1 pound fresh baby spinach, washed
1 watercress bunch, washed and trimmed
1 medium-size red onion, thinly sliced in circles
1 cup sliced radishes, crisp
½ pound Stilton cheese, cut into small pieces or crumbled

DRESSING
8 tablespoons virgin olive oil
4 tablespoons cider vinegar
Salt and freshly ground pepper

1 Dry spinach and watercress well and combine them in a large salad bowl. Add onion slices, radishes, and Stilton cheese. Toss evenly.

2 Prepare vinaigrette by thoroughly mixing ingredients. Just before serving, pour vinaigrette over salad. Mix well.

To believe in God is one thing, to know God another. Both in heaven and on earth, the Lord is made known only by the Holy Spirit, and not through ordinary learning.

STARETZ SILUAN

TODAY my neighbors get ready to barbecue and celebrate the Fourth of July holiday in the pleasantness of the outdoors. On these July evenings, the air is filled with appetizing smells from porches and terraces in the neighborhood as people enjoy their meals *al fresco*, benefiting from the extra hours of daylight.

Grilling, I often tell friends, is a delightful technique of preparing food that's most appropriate for longer summer days. Careful barbecuing extracts vibrant flavors from fish and meats and allows vegetables and mushrooms to keep their superb textures. However, hand-in-hand with the main components of a grilled meal is a fresh, quickly tossed salad that completes and enhances the meal. Grilled meat or fish served without a colorful, crunchy salad leaves me lacking.

Rustic salads belong in a category all their own. They tend to be basic, emphasizing the essential ingredients and adding nothing superfluous. Take, for example, the basic green salad. Only the fresh, crisp leaves of greens are used in its preparation. With a touch of a light vinaigrette, the result is a perfect start or finish to a congenial meal.

A rustic salad exudes a special appeal, a unique appearance and flavor. It may have that country look, where the vegetables seem to have just been harvested from the local garden or brought home from a farmer's stand. They're strikingly beautiful in the vividness of their color and texture. Above all, they're easy to assemble.

Some of these rustic salads have the appeal of their mountain origins. *Mont Blanc* potato salad was conceived in the mountains of Savoie and remains a regional speciality. But whatever their origins, these recipes add a new dimension to the world of salads, serving as wonderful alternatives to more popular, predictable salads.

Today, the monastery joins the rest of the country for a glorious observance of Independence Day. We'll have an evening outdoor picnic, celebrating and rejoicing in the company of close friends while watching the colorful displays of fireworks. The salad I prepared for the picnic is a quick one, made essentially of bulgur and seasonal vegetables and herbs.

JULY FOURTH TABOULI SALAD

6–8 SERVINGS

1½ cup bulgur wheat
Cold water
4 tablespoons lemon juice
⅓ cup virgin olive oil
1 small red onion, finely chopped
1 green bell pepper, finely chopped
1 large tomato, peeled and
    finely chopped
1 small fresh cucumber, peeled and
    cubed
⅓ cup fresh Italian parsley,
    finely chopped
⅓ cup fresh mint, finely chopped
Salt and freshly ground pepper

1 Place bulgur in a large casserole with cold water. Let it stand for 1 hour or a bit more. Drain liquid. Place bulgur in a large salad bowl and add lemon juice and olive oil. Mix well.

2 Add remaining ingredients except enough cherry tomatoes and olives to garnish each serving. Mix well, cover bowl, and refrigerate 1 to 2 hours. Serve cold. Scatter a few cherry tomatoes and olives over each serving as garnish.

JULY 11 ◆ An Array of Creative Salads

DURING THESE HOT, sultry July days when time seems to stand still, I take great delight in distinguishing each day from the others with a different salad concoction. No two salads are alike. Even if I repeat the same recipe, the result is almost always a different salad. Salads, like soups, inspire creativity. When we entertain the notion of preparing a salad, we face an enormous variety of produce available year-round as well as their dazzling combinations of colors, textures, and flavors. In deciding among these choices, we must think of the result we wish to achieve.

Today, thanks to the labor of gardeners and farmers and the international distribution of produce, the average supermarket stocks an amazing variety of fruits, vegetables, grains, and cheeses, making it easier for cooks to create a wide array of appealing salads appropriate for any occasion.

Creative salads can become the basis of healthful and nourishing eating habits. Fresh ingredients rich in vitamins and minerals assure we're getting proper nutrients.

*A salad is like
a Spanish inn.
It accepts everyone
and everything
it can hold.*

MARIE-THERESE CARRERAS

As you search for salad ingredients, always choose the best and freshest vegetables, top-quality fruits, low-calorie seafood, fresh eggs, wholesome pasta, hearty grains, and good cheeses, oils, and vinegars.

Today is the day the monastery celebrates the solemnity of our father Saint Benedict. It's a day of the year particularly cherished by monks who live under the inspiration of his *Rule*. Today's fare is festive, a salad that honors Saint Benedict by being plain and simple in its preparation while still retaining its elegance, having its origins in the home of a noble family of Naples, Italy.

FESTIVE SALAD FOR SAINT BENEDICT'S DAY

4 SERVINGS

2 avocados, peeled, halved, and sliced into even pieces
1 fresh lemon, halved
4 ripe tomatoes, sliced into even pieces
8 slices of fresh mozzarella cheese
1 small red onion, thinly sliced in circles
8 tablespoons virgin olive oil
Sea salt and freshly ground pepper
10 fresh basil leaves, finely cut

1 Place avocado slices in a bowl and sprinkle them with the juice from half a lemon.

2 Arrange avocado slices evenly on four serving plates. Add the slices of 1 tomato to each serving. Add 2 mozzarella-cheese slices to each plate. Evenly distribute onion slices over the avocado, tomatoes, and mozzarella.

3 Pour 2 tablespoons of olive oil over the salad. Sprinkle with sea salt and freshly ground pepper. Top with freshly cut basil leaves as garnish and serve immediately.

SAINT BENEDICT'S DAY

A GOOD FRENCH MEAL is not complete without a bowl of salad, a loaf of bread, or a bottle of wine. Often the ordinary French eater orders a salad in a restaurant for the sole purpose of cleansing his or her palate for some of the good things to come: namely, cheeses and desserts.

During the eighteenth century, salad dishes became fashionable among French nobility. Inventive chefs reveled in creating new delicacies for their distinguished clients. During this period, mayonnaise was invented as a new salad dressing.

Years after the French Revolution, the new restaurants that emerged throughout Paris regularly presented salads. Customers reacted favorably to most of these additions, but people who moved from the provinces to the capital began demanding traditional salads from their regions. French cooking has always maintained a regional perspective, and the best dishes originate from local specialties from the provinces. In this, the salad is not an exception.

France's fondness for the salad has become a global fondness. There is more and more demand among international chefs for little-known recipes tucked away

In a good salad, the main ingredients sparkle with their own identity.

AUTHOR UNKNOWN

in the traditions of French-village cuisine. Nutritionists have also discovered the value of these health-giving salad recipes, which are as varied as the regions they represent. The secret, of course, is to prepare them with similar fresh, local ingredients and to pay attention to the nuances of a vinaigrette or dressing. A good salad always starts with the perfect dressing.

POTATO SALAD A LA PROVENÇAL

6–8 SERVINGS

**10 medium-size red potatoes,
   peeled and quartered**
Pinch of sea salt
Freshly ground pepper
3 parsley sprigs, finely chopped
5 tablespoons extra-virgin olive oil
2 teaspoons fresh lemon juice
2 tablespoons olive oil
4 garlic cloves, minced
2 tablespoons honey

1 Boil potatoes in salted water over medium heat 20 to 25 minutes or until potatoes are cooked and tender. Do not overcook. Drain under cold running water and place in a large salad bowl. Let stand 15 or 20 minutes until cool.

2 Add black pepper, parsley, olive oil, and lemon juice. Toss gently.

3 Heat oil in a skillet over medium heat. Add garlic. Sauté for 1 minute, shaking skillet often so garlic doesn't burn. Add honey and continue stirring for just under 1 minute. Add sauce to salad and toss once more. Serve alone or with the main course.

GOD HAS ENDOWED his creation with such marvelous things as eggs, milk, and fish. Each enhances our daily nutrition while inspiring many culinary delights. God has made both the earth and the sea bountiful; how grateful we should indeed be, as we nourish ourselves daily from the gifts of his providence.

Eggs, cheese, and fish are nature's most simple and perfect foods. Their nutritional value, especially as sources of protein, is very high. When we add eggs, cheese, or fish to a mixed-vegetable salad, the result is a complete meal that encompasses all the ingredients of a balanced diet.

During the summer months when the weather makes it uncomfortable to spend time by a hot stove, salad combinations of vegetables, eggs, cheese, and fish are the perfect alternative to a labor-intensive meal. A bowl of fresh greens, succulent red tomatoes, onion, cucumbers, and the last-minute addition of a hard-boiled egg, crumbled blue cheese, or bits of smoked salmon create a meal that will linger in the mind long after it's savored on the tongue.

Salad and eggs,
and lighter fare,
Tune the Italian
spark's guitar.

MATTHEW PRIOR

Today the Catholic Church calendar commemorates the feast of Saint James, an apostle of the Lord and martyr of the faith. The main course for tonight's supper is a simple salad in which five ingredients are the main staples: avocado, eggs, red peppers, onion, and romaine lettuce. This salad is perfectly suited for vegetarians and nonvegetarians alike because it contains enough protein to satisfy both.

SAINT JAMES EGG AND AVOCADO SALAD
6–8 SERVINGS

2 cooled hard-boiled eggs
2 medium-size sweet red peppers,
boiled for 5 minutes and
then peeled
1 small head romaine lettuce, washed,
drained, and cut into bite-size pieces
1 medium-size red onion,
sliced in half moons
2 medium-size avocados,
peeled and sliced in dices
2 tablespoons lemon juice
4 tablespoons mayonnaise,
homemade or commercial
(more if necessary)
Salt and freshly ground pepper

1 Separate egg yolks and whites. Chop whites and place them in a large salad bowl. Add peeled and diced sweet peppers, lettuce, and onion. Toss gently.

2 Place diced avocado into a separate smaller bowl and sprinkle with the juice of half a lemon, the equivalent of 2 tablespoons. Mix gently and add to salad. Add mayonnaise, salt, and pepper to taste. Toss gently.

3 Served in a large salad bowl or on a large platter. Refrigerate for at least 1 hour. Just before serving, sprinkle with crumbled egg yolks as garnish.

The feast of SAINT JAMES

URING THE SUMMER, many of us don't want to fuss too much around a hot kitchen. During the long winter months it feels natural to get into a relaxed mood around a hot stove, but during the summer it's another story. Yet we who enjoy cooking for others must still find a way to do our task creatively, enhance the table, and provide appetizing food to the palate.

Pasta salads, whether eaten at home or a restaurant, are extremely popular on hot summer days. Pasta salads are not only tasty, but economical, thus immensely appealing to a budget-conscious person or family. They're also ideal for a frugal monastic community in which monks' hearty appetites must be satisfied.

Pasta salads are often served at casual picnics or informal buffet dinners. Their ease of preparation gives them an appeal all their own. The pasta can be cooked in advance, sometimes even the day before, and later combined with the remaining ingredients and chilled until being served. Later that day or on the days following, the salad is ready to be eaten on returning from work. This, of course, isn't the case for a pasta salad served at room temperature: here, the pasta must be cooked at the last minute, *al dente,* and then prepared and served.

In all cases, always avoid overcooking the pasta. Pasta must always be *al dente.* Otherwise, it loses its best qualities: firmness and crunchiness. When choosing pasta at the market, I select one made of pure, wholesome grains. It makes an enormous difference in taste and nutritional value.

One ought to rise from a meal able to apply oneself to prayer and study.

SAINT JEROME

Cooking, be it simple or sublime, is a never-ending occupation no matter when it's done. Summer, winter, spring, or fall—people have to eat, and we as cooks must provide for their appetites. This is where salads of all kinds come very handily to our aid, especially during these often brutally hot and humid days.

PASTA AND MUSHROOM SALAD

6–8 SERVINGS

1 pound rotelle or other noodles
2 tablespoons olive oil
Pinch of sea salt
12 medium-size mushroom caps, cleaned and sliced ¼ inch thick
3 shallots, diced, or 1 medium-size red onion, finely chopped
6-ounce can of medium-size pitted ripe black olives, drained
2 sprigs of flat Italian parsley, finely chopped

DRESSING
⅓ cup virgin olive oil
4 tablespoons red-wine vinegar
1 garlic clove, minced
Salt and freshly ground pepper

1 Mix dressing ingredients well and let stand.

2 Prepare noodles according to package directions and adding olive oil and sea salt. Drain noodles under cold running water and place in a large salad bowl.

3 Add shallots, mushrooms, olives, and parsley. Toss lightly.

4 Pour dressing over salad. Mix gently. Cover and refrigerate for at least 1 hour. Serve cold.

SAINT MARTHA'S DAY

PASTA AND MOZZARELLA SALAD

4–6 SERVINGS

8 ounces fusilli or penne pasta

5 ounces smoked mozzarella, cubed

1 roasted red pepper, cut into long thin strips (or a 7-ounce jar of the same)

1 small red onion, cut into long thin strips

1 bunch of fresh arugula, trimmed (substitute watercress if arugula isn't available)

SALAD DRESSING

6 tablespoons olive oil

2 drops red-pepper sauce

2 tablespoons balsamic vinegar

Salt and freshly ground pepper

1 tablespoon lemon juice

1 Cook pasta according to package directions. Rinse it under cold water and drain. Place pasta in a large salad bowl. Add roasted pepper, arugula (substitute watercress if arugula isn't available), mozzarella, and onion.

2 Prepare salad dressing in a small bowl, mix well, and pour over salad. Toss salad and serve. This salad may be served at room temperature or cold (after 1 hour of refrigeration).

AUGUST

*A*UGUST IS THE TIME OF THE YEAR when the sweet scent of the flowers, herbs, and fresh vegetables pervade our garden. I enjoy reflecting on the utter compatibility of our gardens and kitchen: One grows and produces the vegetables to be served, and the other experiments with and blends those products into delights for the palate.

Summer vegetables are easily recognizable for their brilliant colors, well-developed flavors, and exquisite textures and freshness. The most exquisite tomatoes, drenched in the heat from the sun and saturated with vitamins and taste, are harvested. The same goes for other summer vegetables. These factors make a perfect case for preparing salads often on these beastly hot days.

The flavors and crunchiness of our veggies at this time of the year inspire me to rethink how to enhance our salads. Salad making, in general, is uncomplicated. The basic ingredients can easily be assembled at the final moment, thus saving a great deal of time. Just before serving, a quick vinaigrette or dressing can be prepared by hand or in a blender. I tend to be old-fashioned and prepare them by hand except on the rare occasion when a dressing really needs the help of a blender or mixer.

Many of these basic salad recipes can be put together in a few minutes. One can delight in knowing the main course can be easily enhanced by a simple, healthful, attractive salad. With little or no effort, a last-minute improvised salad can raise an ordinary meal to new heights. This is especially true when the freshest ingredients are used, as is the case during the summer months.

The plain-and-simple salad I'm planning for tonight's dinner is inspired by the monastery garden and what it currently contains. Two hours before dinner, I take a quick walk to the garden and, armed with an old basket, I collect the ingredients for the salad. There is plenty to choose from, but I restrain myself and choose only four or five ingredients. It's sufficient for and more than adequate for the salad planned

Strange to see how a good dinner and feasting reconcile everybody.

SAMUEL PEPYS

for tonight. I strongly believe that fresh salads, a gift from the Lord through the bounty of our gardens, make a huge difference in our daily diet.

It's so easy to take these simple things from the garden and transform them into something that makes people appreciate what goes into our bodies. Such ingredients give ultimate meaning to a cuisine that, above all, should be first concerned not only with pleasuring people, but feeding them with the healthiest and very best produce available. The quality of the food should always be the primary concern of any chef, whether their domain be that of a restaurant or any ordinary home.

MONASTERY GARDEN SALAD

4–6 SERVINGS

1 bunch green oak-leaf or other lettuce
1 bunch arugula, trimmed
1 medium cucumber, washed but
    not peeled, thinly sliced
24 cherry tomatoes, washed
1 medium red onion,
    thinly sliced in circles

DRESSING
5 tablespoons virgin olive oil
3 teaspoons fresh lemon juice
2 teaspoons brown sugar
1 teaspoon creamy mustard,
    preferably French
Salt and freshly ground pepper

1 Wash salad ingredients and dry thoroughly. Tear lettuce into bite-size pieces.

2 Combine salad ingredients in a large salad bowl.

3 Whisk dressing in a cup or small bowl for 1 or 2 minutes until well blended. Just before serving, pour dressing over salad and toss well. Serve immediately after main course or a plate of pasta.

Another of my plain-and-simple salad recipes is based mainly on peppers. People find it very attractive when served at a summer buffet or a picnic. I prepared it again two days ago, and it was a great success. Enjoy the succulent flavors of summer!

SALADE AUX TROIS POIVRONS (Three-Pepper Salad)

6 SERVINGS

1 large-size green pepper, cubed
1 large-size red pepper, cubed
1 large-size yellow pepper, cubed
1 medium-size cucumber,
    peeled and cubed
1 red onion, cut into small pieces
8-ounce tin of pitted black olives,
    drained and halved
1 teaspoon fresh lemon juice
1 small bunch fresh parsley,
    washed and minced

VINAIGRETTE

6 tablespoons extra-virgin olive oil
2 tablespoons fresh lemon juice
Salt and freshly ground black pepper

1 Place all vegetables except parsley in a good-size bowl. Add the lemon juice and toss well. Refrigerate about 2 hours.

2 Remove bowl from refrigerator. Blend vinaigrette ingredients well and pour over salad. Add finely minced parsley. Toss salad until ingredients are well mixed.

3 Serve as a side dish to the main course. It goes well with fish, meat, poultry, and egg dishes and any vegetarian dish.

*T*ODAY, WE CELEBRATE the Feast of the Lord's Transfiguration, a preeminently monastic feast and one of the loveliest of the Christian calendar. Monks throughout the ages have identified themselves with the mystery, for the Transfiguration of Christ symbolizes the transformation that must take place in our own lives. During the moment of the Transfiguration, the veil covering his divinity is briefly lifted, and suddenly we see Jesus clothed in the luminous beauty of his glory. He becomes translucent, all beautiful, resplendent with heavenly glory. And from on high we hear the mysterious words: "This is my Son, the Beloved; with him I am well pleased; listen to him!" (Matthew 17:5).

As I ponder the mystery of the Transfiguration within the depths of my heart, I continue my ordinary kitchen duties. In the spirit of the feast, I decide to prepare a festal salad that is deeply rooted in Italian culinary tradition.

The Italians have created innumerable imaginative salad dishes that are a special pride of their cuisine. This shouldn't be surprising: Italy is the country of olive oil and balsamic vinegar—the country whose inhabitants firmly believe youth is renewed by the ingestion of salads.

Most regions of Italy, like those of France or Spain, have a unique salad that is the pride and joy of their cuisine. Unlike in France, where the salad is usually served midcourse or after the main plate, Italians like to serve it as a first course and call it *antipasto* (plural *antipasti*). Antipasto is basically marinated vegetables drizzled with olive oil.

Crisp, raw salads or antipasto salads of cooked vegetables tend to whet the Italian appetite for the tantalizing dishes to come. The antipasto recipes I present here can be served year-round. I never tire of the Lombardian salad, so I prepare it a few times a year. Unfortunately, Belgian endives are rather dear here in the United States, though they are readily available, but this is an excellent salad to serve after the main course.

Every glimpse of God is his gift, to lead us to long more for that most blessed, ever-longing, ever-satisfied knowledge of him, which will be the bliss of eternity.

EDWARD B. PUSEY
(1800–1882)

Feast of the
TRANSFIGURATION

ENDIVE AND GORGONZOLA SALAD FROM LOMBARDY

6–8 SERVINGS

6 medium-size Belgian endives,
   separated into individual leaves
½ cup shelled walnuts, chopped
½ cup Gorgonzola cheese, cut into small pieces
1 medium red onion, peeled and
   thinly sliced in half moons

DRESSING

4 tablespoons extra-virgin olive oil
2 tablespoons heavy or light cream,
   depending on preference
2 tablespoons white-wine or other vinegar
1 tablespoon finely chopped chervil
Salt and white pepper

1 Place endive leaves in a large salad bowl. If leaves are too big, break them into bite-size pieces or in halves. Add walnuts, Gorgonzola cheese, and onion. Toss well.

2 Just before serving, thoroughly blend dressing ingredients until smooth and creamy. Pour dressing over salad and mix well. Serve at room temperature.

Another classic Italian salad I'm rather fond of comes from Sicily: Insalata di Arance. *It represents well the unique cuisine of Sicily, in which different vegetables and fruits are brought together to create a deep and appetizing contrast. Last Sunday I prepared this salad for a group of monastery guests, and they were delighted with it. Here it is, in all its Sicilian charm and simplicity.*

INSALATA DI ARANCE (Sicilian Orange Salad)

6–8 SERVINGS

1 small head of tender curly endive, washed, dried, and cut into bite-size pieces
5 medium-size juicy oranges, peeled and separated
1 red onion, peeled and thinly sliced
1 cup fresh flat Italian parsley, coarsely chopped
1 cup pitted black Sicilian olives
Pinch of sea salt

DRESSING

7 tablespoons extra-virgin olive oil
2 tablespoons red-wine vinegar
½ teaspoon paprika
1 small garlic clove, minced

1 Place endive, oranges, onion, parsley, olives, and sea salt in a good-size salad bowl. Toss gently.

2 In a small bowl, mix dressing ingredients well and let stand for 1 hour. Just before serving, pour dressing over salad and mix lightly. Serve immediately.

THE MONASTIC CALENDAR, like the secular one, is repeated year after year. It waits for no one and always arrives on time. The seasons of the liturgical calendar give us daily occasion to remember God's friends and our intercessors, the saints. No one should be surprised, then, that so many of my recipes bear a saint's name. This is completely natural to me, for each day I think of and pray to the saint whose memory is kept on that date. I keep continual company with the Mother of God and the saints, and I'm inspired by their words and example.

Someone once asked me if there was a special mystical meaning in the recipes that bear the names of saints. She thought the saint had created the recipe. I told her that naming recipes after saints was my way of honoring them and helping others think of them and remember their legacies.

A few years ago I was asked to speak at a library. Afterward, I was invited to supper at the home of one of the library trustees. To my surprise, the meal had been prepared from my own recipes. As she served the salad, the hostess said, "This is Saint Joseph's salad." Someone asked who Saint Joseph was and why I had named this recipe after him. I told everyone that Joseph was Mary's husband and Jesus' foster father and that he is particularly dear to me because of his unfailing protection. Naming the recipe after him was simply a way of thanking him.

Later, one of the other guests said, "Thank you for telling us about Saint Joseph. I'd never heard of him." When I arrived back at the monastery and entered

SAINT LAWRENCE'S DAY

Give me neither poverty nor riches; feed me with the food that I need.

PROVERBS 30:8

the chapel to sing Compline, I gazed at the icon of Saint Joseph with renewed love and devotion. A special aura seemed to pulse from the icon, as if the saint were trying to convey something to me. Perhaps it was a simple thank you for honoring his memory.

Today we celebrate the memory of Saint Lawrence, a deacon and martyr of the early Church who is now the patron saint of deacons. He was well known for his care and devotion to the poor, the elderly, and widows. Tonight's salad is colorful, making use of red tomatoes to remind us of Saint Lawrence's martyrdom. May this faithful friend of Christ, a young witness and martyr for the cause of the Gospel, continue to bless daily all our kitchen endeavors. The Saints are not only God's friends but also ours. As such, I count much on their help, their example of Christian living, and especially on their intercession during our own earthly journey to God.

SAINT LAWRENCE SALAD

6–8 SERVINGS

1 small head Romaine lettuce, washed and drained, cut into bite-size pieces
20 cherry tomatoes, washed and halved
10 mushrooms, sliced
6-ounce can of pitted black olives, rinsed and drained
1 small onion, finely chopped
A few fresh basil leaves, coarsely chopped

DRESSING
8 tablespoons extra-virgin olive oil
¼ cup lemon juice
1 egg yolk
¼ teaspoon nutmeg
1 teaspoon sugar
Salt and freshly ground pepper

1 Combine lettuce, tomatoes, mushrooms, olives, and onion in a deep salad bowl. Toss lightly. Refrigerate for at least 1 hour before serving.

2 In a blender, combine dressing ingredients and whirl until it thickens and achieves an even consistency. Refrigerate until ready to use.

3 Arrange salad on individual plates. Just before serving, pour dressing on top. Top with chopped basil as garnish. Serve immediately. This salad can be served as an appetizer or after the main course.

DURING THESE quiet mid August summer days, it's still light when we sing our daily Compline at about 8 PM. In France, they used to say midsummer is the year's middle age, for once we reach this glorious Assumption festivity, we seem to have reached a time of fullness and completion. This sense of fullness is very appropriate for today, as we celebrate the completion and crowning of the earthly life of Mary, the Mother of God. Today, in honor of her feast, I look at my humble and small repertoire of exotic salads for inspiration. Nothing is more appetizing and calming on a hot, sultry summer night than a healthy and fresh salad whose main elements spring from our own garden. These so-called exotic salads are unique in their preparation and place of origin, and they're a welcome variation on our usual salad concoctions.

Salads range from simple and humble to sophisticated and exotic. Salads that come from the French culinary tradition, for instance, are known for their inventiveness and refinement. Some of these exotic salads aren't part of our habitual monastic diet, which tends toward the simple and frugal. As a cook I can't utterly ignore them, so from time to time I experiment with the most uncomplicated ones, deliberately limiting my selection to the few I've been exposed to throughout the years.

Exotic salads reveal not only hidden cultural aspects of other culinary traditions, but also the immense possibilities that exist for salad-making. One thing we can all learn from these salads is that they're always open to change and transformation. What sometimes begins with basic and simple ingredients may become, through

*God, who
made the earth,
The air, the sky,
the sea,
Who gave
the light its birth,
Careth for me.*

SARAH BETTS RHODES
(1829–1904)

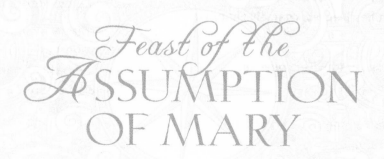

Feast of the
ASSUMPTION
OF MARY

subtle alterations, a very exotic dish. The art of salad-making contains many secrets, and the artful chef must discover their many configurations.

The summer months give us ample time to experiment with the creation of new salad dishes. August, a month in which I don't want to spend too much time around a hot stove, is a great time to try tantalizing salad recipes. One of the so-called exotic salads I often enjoy preparing is a simple and basic salad that originated in Morocco. Yes, it's a bit exotic, and by that I mean it has an unusual flavor, but the result is always an added delight to the palette. It's one of the few salads in which salt isn't used, and it's particularly striking for its sweet taste. Here's the recipe in its most basic form.

MOROCCAN SALAD
6–8 SERVINGS

1 head Boston, Bibb, or other tender green
  leaf lettuce, washed and drained
1 cup pitted dates, halved lengthwise
5 clementine oranges, peeled, segments separated
4 medium-size beets, boiled, peeled, and cubed
1 small red onion, finely chopped

DRESSING
4 tablespoons extra-virgin olive oil
2 tablespoons fresh orange juice
2 tablespoons white-wine vinegar
2 tablespoons raw or white sugar
⅓ teaspoon liquid hot-pepper seasoning or
  freshly ground black pepper

1 Tear lettuce into bite-size pieces and place them in a large salad bowl. Add dates, oranges, precooked beets, and onion. Toss lightly.

2 1 hour before serving, mix dressing ingredients well. Let stand until ready to serve.

3 Just before serving, pour dressing over salad and toss gently until all elements are evenly coated. Serve immediately.

*A*T ONE TIME vegetables and fruits were never mixed in the same bowl. I was raised with this culinary stigma. It's hard to believe now, because today people all over the world combine all sorts of produce to create nourishing salads. The blending of fruit and vegetables allows the chef to enrich the salad bowl with diverse textures, subtle flavors, and a range of decorative colors. Who can resist the appeal of limitless combinations?

Fruit salads are a favorite lunch or brunch for many people, especially in hot weather. They're light, tasty, and always refreshing. There's no reason, however, why fruit can't be included in the evening salad as an appetizer, side dish, or accessory to the main course.

Always choose the freshest seasonal fruit and avoid canned or frozen fruit, even in the midst of winter. Also, be mindful of the dressing when combining fruit and vegetables or when using fruit alone. The right dressing is the secret to a good salad—it can either enhance it or destroy it.

In August, all sorts of fruits combined with salad greens are my preferred choices for a nutritious and colorful salad. I enjoy mixing the textures and flavors of fruits with the more subtle and delicate taste of greens and vegetables such as beets. Citrus fruits, apples, pears, and peaches mix wonderfully with mild greens and other vegetables, enhancing contrasting flavors.

These recipes originated in our monastery kitchen and are often recreated during the summer. Today the entire monastic family honors Saint Bernard, a remarkable monk and one of the most influential people in the Middle Ages. Our special vegetable-fruit salad is named after him.

The fruit of the land shall be the pride and glory of the survivors of Israel.

ISAIAH 4:2

Feast of
SAINT BERNARD

SPINACH AND FRUIT SALAD

6–8 SERVINGS

1 pound baby spinach, washed and dried

1 medium-size red onion, thinly sliced

6 large-size tangerines (or clementine oranges),
    peeled, segments separated

4 peaches, peeled and evenly sliced

1 mango, pitted, peeled, and cut into chunks

DRESSING

8 tablespoons extra-virgin olive oil

4 tablespoons lemon juice

2 tablespoons sugar

1 teaspoon dry mustard

Salt

1 Arrange spinach and onion on a large platter or in individual salad plates.

2 Place fruits in a salad bowl and toss gently.

3 Blend dressing ingredients well. Just before serving, pour dressing over fruit and toss to coat.

4 Place fruit on spinach bed and serve. (If prepared ahead of time, mixed fruit can be refrigerated.)

KIWI AND BANANA SALAD

6–8 SERVINGS

4 apples, peeled, cored, and thinly sliced

4 bananas, sliced

1 cup green grapes

6 kiwi fruit, peeled and evenly sliced crosswise

1 cup walnuts

DRESSING

½ cup plain yogurt

⅓ cup mayonnaise

3 tablespoons honey

2 teaspoons lemon juice

½ teaspoon nutmeg

1 Combine fruit and walnuts in a large salad bowl and refrigerate until ready to use.

2 Just before serving, mix dressing ingredients in a bowl. Blend well and pour over fruit. Toss gently and serve.

THE FRENCH SAY a good salad starts with a good dressing. Vinaigrettes—and salad dressings in general—are meant to enhance the taste and presentation of the salad. They go a long way toward making dramatic, memorable salads that won't soon be forgotten.

Vinaigrette has deep biblical origins. Salt, oil, and vinegar can be found throughout both Old and New Testaments. Salt and oil are symbols of life used in the ritual of the sacraments of baptism and confirmation. They're also rich symbols of taste, power, and unction, and as such they're life-giving. It's not surprising, therefore, to see how these elements have become the main ingredients or components of any basic salad dressing.

Basic salad dressings and sauces tend to be few in number, but they lend themselves to infinite variations. The basic French vinaigrette—good olive oil, wine vinegar (*le mariage de l'huile et la vinaigre*), and salt and pepper to taste—offers endless possibilities the moment you start adding ingredients, be they minced garlic clove, a teaspoon of Dijon mustard, a handful of finely chopped fresh herbs, or a combination of honey and mustard. The same can be said of mayonnaise: Add a few minced garlic cloves and you have an aioli; add extra Dijon or Meaux mustard and you create a *sauce remoulade*. With vinaigrettes, dressings, and sauces, any creative chef can reinvent recipes to give the magic touch to a salad.

Vinaigrettes, dressings, and sauces are sold commercially. Although they simplify the task of

You are the salt of the earth; but if salt has lost its taste, how can its saltiness be restored?

MATTHEW 5:13

the cook, they cannot in any way compare to the wonders of a homemade dressing or vinaigrette. Commercial dressings should be relegated to emergencies such as the feeding of a large crowd.

To prepare a good dressing or vinaigrette, start with the best ingredients: high-quality olive oil, a refined type of vinegar, sea salt, and freshly ground pepper. Additional ingredients should also be fresh: lemons, fresh eggs for mayonnaise, fresh herbs, or quality dry herbs when fresh are not available.

Most dressings, sauces, and vinaigrettes can be prepared ahead and refrigerated (my aioli mayonnaise is an exception). There's nothing mysterious about a good dressing or sauce; the chef simply needs a good amount of creativity and ingenuity to impart a gourmet flavor to a salad that may otherwise be a penny-wise cost.

Many of the vinaigrettes, dressings, and sauces in this book are included in the recipes for the salads. What follows here are the basic and often-used recipes that inspire other varieties.

ROQUEFORT DRESSING

MAKES ²/₃ CUP

¼ cup low-fat sour cream
¼ cup heavy cream
2 tablespoons olive oil
2 tablespoons white-wine vinegar
Salt and white pepper
2 ounces of Roquefort cheese, crumbled

1 Combine all ingredients except cheese in a deep bowl. Beat with an electric mixer until dressing is smooth and creamy.

2 Add crumbled cheese and mix well with a fork or spoon. Refrigerate for several hours before using.

AIOLI MAYONNAISE

1 CUP

2 very fresh egg yolks
4 garlic cloves, minced
1 tablespoon fresh lemon juice or
    tarragon vinegar
1 teaspoon Dijon mustard
Salt and white pepper
1 cup light olive oil or vegetable oil

1 The day you plan to use it, put egg yolks in a deep bowl. Add garlic, lemon juice, and mustard, season with salt and pepper, and mix with a whisk or electric mixer until uniform and creamy (it's simpler and quicker with a mixer).

2 Add 1 teaspoonful of oil at a time, whisking or mixing until the aioli has thickened. Refrigerate until ready to use, but use it the day you prepare it.

CLASSIC VINAIGRETTE

½ CUP

1 teaspoon salt
½ teaspoon freshly ground
    black pepper
2 tablespoons red-wine vinegar
6 tablespoons extra-virgin olive oil

1 Put salt, pepper, and vinegar in a measuring cup or bowl and stir thoroughly. Add oil and stir until ingredients are blended.

2 *Vinaigrette with mustard:* Prepare classic vinaigrette, then whisk in 1 tablespoon of Dijon, Meaux, or other French mustard and mix thoroughly.

3 *Vinaigrette with herbs:* Prepare classic vinaigrette, substituting fresh lemon juice for vinegar. Add ¼ cup finely chopped fresh herbs of your choice (such as parsley, tarragon, or cilantro) or scallions. Mix thoroughly.

BLENDED CAESAR DRESSING

1 CUP

1 egg
½ cup grated Romano or
    Parmesan cheese
4 tablespoons lemon juice
2 garlic cloves, minced
1 teaspoon Worcestershire sauce
Salt and pepper
12 tablespoons olive oil

1 Combine all ingredients except olive oil in a blender.

2 Whirl until well blended. With the blender still on, add olive oil at a slow, steady pace until thoroughly blended. Refrigerate until ready to use.

SEPTEMBER

Labor Day Picnic

AS WE REACH the long Labor Day weekend, we're deeply mindful that summer is beginning to wane and that we're steering toward the completion of the season. It's a time of transition, and a certain magic in the air brings back memories of previous summers. Our thoughts return to vacations by the beach, picnics in the countryside or woods or mountains. We can almost taste the fresh, crunchy cheese-filled baguette we shared that day with family and friends, almost hear and smell the intermingling of melody and sweet air at an outdoor concert.

But Labor Day is about more than the end of summer. It's an exciting new beginning for youngsters returning to school or attending classes for the first time. It's also about honoring the work force—the people who toil daily to put food on the table and bring prosperity to their families and communities. What would our world be today without them? We owe so much to the working men and women of the world. They cooperate with the Creator to make our world a better and safer place to live. May the Lord in his goodness continue to bless the work of their hands.

Here in the monastery, we celebrate the weekend with an appetizing picnic on

our porch with its glorious view of our barn, gardens, and of course the surrounding fields. A simple picnic is so gratifying, a good time to gather with some of our closest friends to celebrate the abundance of our garden, where all sorts of late vegetables and herbs have begun to render their fruits: eggplants, fava beans, squash, potatoes, and tomatoes in great quantities this year because of the amount of rain we've received over the summer.

Picnic food is casual, fresh, appetizing, and uncomplicated. Picnic food springs from the heart, from the season, from the

A French picnic, as a rule, tends to be a simple affair— little more than a jug of wine, a loaf of bread, and thou.

CRAIG PYES

garden, and from the gift of good weather and the outdoors as it invites us to relaxed entertaining and good cheer. When the picnic is at home, barbecuing or grilling can play an integral role in food preparation. The grill on our porch is put to good use during picnics.

These recipes were part of this year's Labor Day picnic. This is a wonderful dip at any time of year, but especially during the summer when eggplants are in season. In Provence, this dip is known as the "poor man's caviar" because anyone can afford it. I usually serve this appetizing dip on slices of French baguette. It also works well on any cracker.

EGGPLANT CAVIAR DIP
8–10 SERVINGS

1 large eggplant
½ cup extra-virgin olive oil
1 large Spanish or Vidalia onion,
    minced
2 medium green peppers,
    chopped into small pieces
4 garlic cloves, minced
1 bay leaf
Salt and freshly ground pepper
3 tablespoons white vermouth
    or dry white wine
1 tablespoon lemon juice

1 Bake eggplant at 350° F for 45 minutes. Allow it to cool, peel it, and chop it coarsely.

2 Pour olive oil into a frying pan and add eggplant and remaining vegetables. Sauté over low-medium heat until mixture turns soft and tender.

3 Add salt and pepper to taste, wine, lemon juice, and bay leaf and simmer gently over low heat 12 to 15 minutes until mixture turns thick and even. Remove bay leaf. Refrigerate at least 2 hours before serving.

POTATO-APPLE-CELERY SALAD

8–10 SERVINGS

2 pounds new small potatoes, peeled and halved
1 pound Macintosh apples, peeled and thinly sliced
3 celery stalks, thinly sliced
1 medium-size red onion, finely chopped
A few sprigs of fresh parsley, finely chopped

DRESSING
½ cup extra-virgin olive oil
4 tablespoons white-wine vinegar
3 tablespoons heavy cream or half-and-half
1 teaspoon lemon juice
Salt and freshly ground pepper

1 Boil new potatoes in salted water for 15 minutes or until tender. Rinse and drain under cold running water. Place in a large salad bowl. Add apples, celery, onion, and the parsley.

2 Mix dressing ingredients in a blender, jar, or small bowl. Pour over salad and toss. Check seasonings and adjust accordingly. Refrigerate for at least 2 hours before serving. Serve cold.

GRILLED SUMMER SQUASH AND ZUCCHINI

6–8 SERVINGS

½ cup olive oil
1 tablespoon fresh rosemary, minced
1 tablespoon fresh thyme, crushed
3 garlic cloves, minced
1 tablespoon lemon juice
3 tablespoons balsamic vinegar
Sea salt and freshly ground pepper
4 medium-size zucchini, halved lengthwise
4 medium-size summer squash, halved lengthwise

1 Prepare sauce by combining olive oil, herbs, garlic, lemon juice, vinegar, salt, and pepper in a deep bowl. Mix well.

2 Coat zucchini and squash halves on both sides with a kitchen brush.

3 Grill 3 to 4 minutes per side or until mildly cooked. Serve immediately with main course.

This recipe also works perfectly with eggplants. The sauce recipe makes enough for 4 to 6 medium-size eggplants, the so-called Japanese sort, which are a bit smaller and easier to grill in halves.

GRILLED PITAS WITH TOMATOES AND MOZZARELLA

6 SERVINGS

6 medium-size tomatoes, diced
½ cup pitted black olives, chopped
1 large-size red onion,
    coarsely chopped
6 tablespoons extra-virgin olive oil
6 tablespoons fresh basil, chopped
Sea salt
6 pieces of whole-wheat pita bread
⅔ cup mozzarella cheese,
    cut into small pieces

1 Combine tomatoes, olives, onions, 3 tablespoons of the olive oil, basil, and salt in a large bowl. Stir well and blend.

2 Use a brush to coat 1 side of each pita with remaining olive oil. Place pitas on grill, oily side down. Cook 2 to 3 minutes, but don't let them burn. Turn pitas over and spread tomato–onion mixture evenly over each pita, then sprinkle with cheese. Cover barbecue and continue grilling pitas until cheese melts. Place pitas on plates and serve.

*T*HESE ARE BLESSED DAYS in the garden, a time of reaping the fruits of our summer labors. It's also a special period in the monastic kitchen: a time of intensive food preparation and food preservation for the coming winter. Some days I'm overwhelmed by the enormous amount of work this all entails.

We had a very rainy summer season, and the vegetables and fruits that ordinarily need extra water greatly profited—the humble tomato, for example. I'm delighted with our garden's superabundance of tomatoes. We've been serving them at the table every day and selling them at the Millbrook Farmers' Market, canning and freezing them in sauce form, and making a great deal of salsa.

Nothing captures the flavor of summer like a well-ripened tomato. A home-grown tomato pulls more flavor out of the soil; it delivers a quality of taste, a certain smoothness and texture to which there is no equal. Once they're harvested, you must quickly decide what you're going to do with them. If you're going to freeze them or make tomato sauce, you must do so while the fruit is wholesome, fresh, and ripe. It's the only way to preserve those magical tastes of summer. I add an extra amount of fresh basil just before sealing the jars to enhance the flavor of the sauce and preserve it for good use throughout the winter months.

Today is also the beautiful feast of the Nativity of Mary, a feast that takes me back to Provence and the many Septembers I spent there. Ah, Provence. I can almost feel and smell the aromatic herbs you step on while walking and hiking. The Provençals rely heavily, as many Mediterraneans do, on the tomato for many of their culinary delights. The native cuisine is rather light, distinctive in flavors and textures, and considered one of the most healthy in the world, hence the importance the Provençals attach to the tomato. Their tomato dishes may be enjoyed hot or cold—you need only add a bit of fresh onion, garlic, olive oil, and world-renowned *herbes de Provence*, particularly basil, to end up with a succulent plate preferred to none.

One of the tomato products I'm making today in preparation for the upcoming winter is *tomato coulis*, which is similar to Italian or Spanish tomato sauce yet has distinct characteristics. Coulis is closer to a compote than a sauce. Its consistency and flavor come from the combination of tomatoes, extra-virgin olive oil, shallots or onions, garlic, sea salt, ground pepper, sugar, parsley, and a bay leaf. The *herbes de Provence* (rosemary, thyme) typical to so many regional dishes are deliberately absent in this recipe. Coulis has multiple uses: It can replace the typical tomato sauce, for example, or it can be used in soups, omelettes, and pasta and rice dishes.

Nature does nothing in vain.

ENGLISH PROVERB

COULIS DE TOMATES (Tomato Coulis)

10 tablespoons extra-virgin olive oil

5 shallots or one large Spanish or
    Vidalia onion

5 garlic cloves, peeled and minced

24 medium ripe tomatoes, peeled,
    seeded, and coarsely chopped

A few parsley sprigs, finely chopped

1 bay leaf

Sea salt and freshly ground pepper

1 tablespoon sugar

1 Pour olive oil into a good-size saucepan. Add shallots or onion and sauté lightly over low-medium heat 4 to 5 minutes or until vegetables turn tender. Stir continuously. Add chopped tomatoes, chopped parsley, and bay leaf. Cover saucepan and cook over medium heat for 15 to 20 minutes. Stir from time to time so it doesn't burn.

2 Season with salt, ground pepper, and sugar. Continue cooking for 1 or 2 more minutes, stirring frequently. Remove coulis from heat. Remove bay leaf and discard. Place coulis in two 32-ounce well-sterilized jars and close lid tightly. Boil jars in water for 20 to 30 minutes. Remove jars from heat. Allow them to cool for about 24 hours, then store.

Another tomato Provençal sauce, sauce vierge, *is appreciated in the monastic kitchen during these harvest days. This fresh, raw sauce is very handy during the last days of summer, especially with any pasta dish. It's also excellent over certain types of fish like tuna, and it always enhances a good omelette when used as topping. When served with an omelette, it reminds me a bit of the* Piperade *from the Basque country in the Pyrenees.*

SAUCE VIERGE A LA PROVENÇAL (Fresh Tomato Sauce)

6–8 SERVINGS

7 tablespoons extra-virgin olive oil

10 medium-size ripe tomatoes (pepper tomatoes
    are perfect), peeled, seeded, coarsely chopped

4 garlic cloves, minced

1 small onion or shallot, minced

2 tablespoons lemon juice

10 pitted black olives, coarsely chopped

Sea-salt and freshly ground pepper

12 fresh basil leaves, chopped

2 Italian parsley sprigs, chopped

1 In a stainless-steel casserole or large bowl, combine olive oil, tomatoes, garlic, onion or shallot, lemon juice, and olives. Add salt and ground pepper to taste.

2 Set sauce aside for 3 to 4 hours to allow the rich flavors to blend. Just before serving, add fresh basil and parsley. Mix well. Serve over pasta, fish, or omelette.

Feast of the NATIVITY OF MARY

SEPTEMBER is a wonderful month. Those of us who work and farm spend considerable time gathering the fruits of our spring and summer labors. When I go into the vegetable garden, I bring several large baskets to gather the ripe tomatoes, beans, beets, peppers, eggplants, cucumbers, and onions. This year's crops are of excellent quality, for with the Lord's blessing the land has rendered us a good harvest. I just hope and pray we don't have an early frost and that we continue reaping the garden's yield well into November and even early December.

One regular activity throughout September is to offer our produce and kitchen wares at the local farmers' market. For years we had a booth at the Saturday market where we sold fresh produce and jams, dips, vinegars, herbs, and sauces. We had to stop doing the market every week and now return only occasionally. It's always a joy to see our friends the farmer vendors and the warm clientele and to exchange ideas and results with people interested in farming and food. The salsa we make from the following recipe sells very well.

As the flower is before the fruit, so is faith before good works.

RICHARD WHATELY

FRESH MONASTERY SALSA

MAKES APPROXIMATELY 4 CUPS

6 tomatoes, chopped into
** very small pieces**
1 medium white onion,
** diced into tiny pieces**
1 15-ounce can black beans,
** rinsed and drained**
1 ear of cooked corn, or 1 can
** if no fresh available, drained**
1 small bunch parsley
1 small bunch cilantro
1 small bunch chervil (if available)
1 teaspoon cumin
½ teaspoon cayenne pepper
Red-pepper flakes
Salt and pepper

OPTIONAL:
1 SMALL JALAPENO PEPPER

1 In a large bowl, combine tomatoes, onion, black beans, corn, and if desired, jalapeno.

2 In a small food processor or blender, finely chop parsley, cilantro, and chervil until they have a uniform, pestolike consistency. Add these herbs to the bowl with cumin, cayenne pepper, red-pepper flakes, and salt and pepper. Stir well. Taste and add spices as needed.

3 Spoon salsa into small containers with lids. Refrigerate until ready to eat.

DURING THE MORNING OFFICE, I couldn't help but thank God for the inestimable gift of life. Our world traverses such a dark period these days that life, this precious gift from God, is taken almost for granted. As a Christian monk I am totally opposed to war. The Gospel I believe in is a Gospel of peace that opposes war, violence, and killing in all instances. We need the courage to globalize solidarity and peace. Every day, I invoke peace from God, that peace humankind is not capable of giving. Peace never requires violence—it calls for dialogue. War throws open the doors to the abyss of evil. War makes anything possible, even the totally irrational. War should always be considered defeat, the defeat of reason and humanity.

Saint Francis, whose feast we celebrate in a few weeks, used to pray daily, "Lord, make me an instrument of your peace." He was not a politician, and neither am I. Saint Francis learned from the Gospel to be a messenger of peace. He encouraged everyone to renounce violence at all cost, at every occasion, and in every form. Saint Francis found his strength to follow Jesus' radical pacifism in the consoling words from the Gospel: "Blessed are the peacemakers, for they will be called children of God."

I am called not only to pray that peace prevails in our world, but also to act or speak against every form of violence here at home or abroad. I also must keep myself peaceful and avoid conflict or at least seek a peaceful resolution to any conflict around me. Violence doesn't always start miles away—sometimes it starts in our own homes and in our own hearts. The peacemaker must remain alert to be sure his or her actions encourage others to walk in the ways of peace.

As I ponder and reflect on the reality of peace and the harshness of violence, I notice how quickly the foliage on the monastic property is changing. The dazzling colors beginning to appear in our maple trees are a harbinger of a gorgeous autumn.

These changes in foliage always coincide with harvest season. Indeed, the harvest must be attended to in earnest. I've been picking potatoes steadily for the last three

Lord, make me an instrument of your peace.

SAINT FRANCIS OF ASSISI

days, and I'm far from finished. I've also gone apple-picking at a friend's orchard. Harvest festivals are taking place in Dutchess County and surrounding counties. Everyone wishes to celebrate and feast on the earth's bounty.

Today my kitchen work concentrates on making large quantities of soup. Later I'll preserve it in jars for the winter. I call this soup Monastery Harvest Soup, for it contains almost every vegetable ripening in our garden: potatoes, Swiss chard, leeks, carrots, tomatoes, garlic, zucchini, winter squash, cauliflower, pole beans, celery, and parsley. This never-ending job keeps me laboring in the kitchen for many extra hours.

The soup itself is basic and easy to make—it's the washing and slicing of the vegetables that takes time. Here is the basic recipe.

MONASTERY HARVEST SOUP

2 GALLONS

10 tablespoons olive oil
8 medium-size tomatoes, chopped coarsely
7 garlic cloves, chopped
2 gallons water
2 leeks, white and tender green parts,
  thinly sliced
5 celery stalks, thinly sliced
3 potatoes, peeled and cubed
4 medium-size carrots, peeled and cubed
2 zucchini, cubed
1 winter squash, peeled and cubed
4 Swiss chard leaves, coarsely chopped
1 small cauliflower,
  cut into small pieces
24 or more flat pole beans, shelled
1 bunch of parsley, finely chopped
Sea salt and freshly ground pepper

1 Pour olive oil into an extra-large (more than 2 gallons) soup pot or kettle. If you don't have a large kettle, pour equal amounts into 2 large (over 1 gallon) kettles.

2 Put tomatoes and garlic in a blender or food processor. Blend well 1 to 2 minutes. Pour mixture over oil and heat on low-medium. Stir continuously 2 to 3 minutes so it doesn't burn.

3 Add water and raise heat to medium-high. Add vegetables and bring water to a quick boil. After 20 minutes, lower heat to medium (if too hot, low-medium), cover pot, and let it simmer about 30 minutes. Add sea salt and ground pepper to taste. Check and adjust seasonings. Serve hot or place in large, sterilized jars and boil.

September
is the month
of the migration
of birds, of the
finished harvest,
of nut-gatherings,
of cider making,
and towards
the conclusion,
of the change
of color in the trees.
Its noblest nature
is a certain
festive abundance
for the supply
of all creation.

LEIGH HUNT

TODAY'S EQUINOX marks the first day of autumn. Looking back, I realize summer wasn't easy: the intense labor in the farm and in the gardens, the worry about our crops, the mowing of the lawns, the cutting and splitting of wood for use during the winter. Each of us here in the monastery—monks and guests—went about our daily tasks, preparing ourselves for the eventuality of winter. No matter how pleasant the summer or how lovely and cozy the autumn, the dusk of winter hovers. Sooner or later, reality sinks in and we must confront winter's not too distant arrival. From spring on, we labor and go forward, always preparing for our often harsh northeastern winters. Daily monastic life is very much shaped by the order of the seasons. I wouldn't know what to do in places where the seasons reverse or there are only two seasons. I'd probably end up confused, lost.

When fall makes its entrance, I'm grateful for the quiet and reflective character of autumn: its shorter days and lovely, crisp, clear evenings, its harvest moon hinting at the arrival of the season that crowns the year with such dramatic changes and colors.

In monasteries as in neighboring farms and homes, fall indicates a new round of seasonal activities consisting mostly of the harvest work and preparations for the cold. Bushels of new potatoes, squash, onions, and apples must be stored safely in our cellars. Continuous canning, preserving, and freezing is followed by the harvesting and drying of herbs that will be used in the kitchen during the winter and our vinegar production for the Millbrook vineyards and the extra we'll sell at boutiques and in our small monastic shop. Since the quality of our vinegar was discovered by others, demand for it has grown from an outstanding restaurant in New York City.

Monks, by the very nature of our monastic lives, are dedicated

to the work and stewardship of the land. We live by the immutable rhythms of the seasons, so in the fall we're obliged to set aside other worthwhile occupations and concentrate on the ever-demanding harvest.

Work in the kitchen also has a strong fall flavor. So many of our dishes portray the season's character, the sort of maturity fall implies. There is both a serenity and a rare beauty in our seasonal food. Many of my dishes are inspired by past autumns in Provence.

One of my favorite soups for this time of year is a Provençal soup, *soupe d'Epeautre*. It's basically a barley and chickpea soup wonderfully enhanced with the flavors of Provence. The original recipe calls for a variety of meats. I deliberately avoid the meat and simplify the recipe, giving it a total vegetarian character. That's how soup is prepared in Provençal monasteries, and it's also a healthier rendition of the original. The recipe demands both barley and chickpeas, and I highly recommend they be soaked overnight in separate saucepans or casseroles. If the soup is prepared at the last minute, substitute dried chickpeas for canned.

SOUPE D'EPEAUTRE (Barley-Chickpea Soup)

4–6 SERVINGS

1½ cups barley (or cracked wheat if available)
1 cup chickpeas
2 cups diced pumpkin, peeled and cubed
   (or other available squash)
2 medium-size carrots, peeled and cubed
3 fresh celery stalks, thinly sliced
3 shallots, coarsely chopped
3 garlic cloves, minced
4 dried sage leaves, crushed and crumbled
½ teaspoon dried thyme
1 vegetable bouillon cube
Sea salt and freshly ground pepper
Olive oil
A few sprigs of Italian parsley, finely chopped

1 Pour 12 cups of water into a large soup kettle or saucepan. Add barley, chickpeas, vegetables, garlic, herbs, and bouillon. Salt and pepper to taste. Bring soup to a slow boil over medium–high heat.

2 After 10 minutes, lower heat to low–medium, stir soup once or twice, cover, and let simmer gently for 2 hours. Add water or vegetable stock if necessary. Taste and adjust seasonings as necessary.

3 Top with a dash of olive oil and a sprinkle of finely chopped parsley as garnish. Serve hot.

O N THIS RADIANT, clear, sunny fall day, the autumn scenery along our country roads has become brighter and more intense. The fall foliage is well underway: The elms are growing rusty, the white paniculata by the monastery entrance is in full bloom, the lovely cornflowers and asters are at the peak of their glory, and the maples are turning fiery red, orange, and yellow.

Work in the garden continues daily, though at a lesser pace than that of summer. Autumn is usually the best time to divide and transplant perennials and to plant bulbs for next spring. Here at the monastery, it's also when we bring plants and herbs into the greenhouse so they survive winter. In winter, the greenhouse becomes a true haven of greenery and aromatic scents.

The liturgy has its own rhythm of feasts, seasons, and celebrations. Today we celebrate the Feast of Saint Michael and the Archangels. Archangels are often mentioned in Scripture because the Lord used them frequently as messengers. As true witnesses and worshipers of God, they recall for us God's infinite transcendence and holiness and thus invite us to worship and adore God. Since today is a monastic feast, I decided to honor Saint Michael, Saint Gabriel, and Saint Raphael with a special meal that will use the great amount of tomatoes we're harvesting in the garden: pasta with arrabbiata sauce. Tonight's arrabbiata sauce is spicy, for it makes use of a hot jalapeno or serrano pepper. You only want to serve this sauce to those who enjoy spicy food.

The dessert is inspired by the great apple and pear harvest going on in the Hudson Valley. The apple trees through-

If you eat goose on Michaelmas Day, you will never want money all the year around.

OLD ENGLISH PROVERB

out the valley are filled with luscious fruits: red, yellow, and green apples of all sizes. Recently I visited a friend who generously allowed me to pick any amount of apples on the ground. "Pick as many baskets as you can," he said, "I know you'll put them to good use." Who could refuse such an offer? Certainly not a monk and cook of frugal convictions!

PASTA WITH ARRABBIATA SAUCE

6–8 SERVINGS

SAUCE
3 pounds plum tomatoes, halved
1 fresh hot chile pepper, finely chopped
1 small shallot or white onion, finely chopped
2 garlic cloves, minced
½ cup fresh basil leaves, chopped
8 tablespoons extra-virgin olive oil
Sea salt and freshly ground pepper

1 Place all ingredients except basil in a good-size saucepan. Simmer over low-medium heat, stirring from time to time until sauce thickens, about 30 minutes.

2 When sauce is done, add basil and continue cooking for 1 extra minute. Whirl sauce through a blender or food processor. Keep it warm until it's ready to use.

PASTA
1 pound penne or other pasta
2 teaspoons olive oil
Sea salt

1 Cook pasta in a large sauce pan of salted boiling water. Boil for a few minutes until tender, making sure pasta remains *al dente*. Drain water.

2 Just before serving, toss pasta with arrabbiata sauce and serve immediately. Pass around a bowl of freshly grated Parmesan or other cheese for garnish.

THE ARCHANGELS' DESSERT
(Apples and Pears Poached in Wine and Cider)
10 SERVINGS

5 apples, firm, peeled
5 Anjou pears, peeled
2 cups apple cider
2 cups cranberry juice
2 cups Port or similar wine
1 cup sugar
8 cloves
1 cinnamon stick
1 small piece of fresh ginger
1 strip of lemon or orange zest

1 In a large Dutch oven or other large ovenproof covered dish, stand apples and pears next to each other. Apples and pears should be evenly interspersed.

2 Pour cider, cranberry juice, and wine into a good-size saucepan. Add sugar and bring to a quick boil. Stir continuously so sugar dissolves completely. Reduce heat to low–medium and add spices. Cover and simmer gently for about 15 minutes.

3 Preheat oven to 350° F. Pour liquid over apples and pears. Be sure spices don't rise to the top of the liquid. Cover and place Dutch oven or dish in oven for 25 to 30 minutes. Check from time to time to see that liquid hasn't evaporated. When it's done, only 1 or 2 inches of liquid should remain.

4 Discard spices before serving. Serve at room temperature. Ladle apples and pears into serving dishes, being careful so they don't fall apart. Pour leftover syrup on the top. Serve one apple or pear per person.

OCTOBER

I WOKE UP EARLY on this gentle feast of our guardian angels and opened the door to let fresh air into the kitchen. There is much joy in the loveliness of these early October days. The air is so pure, the skies are so clear, and the ivy in our trees is turning fiery red. No matter where I rest my gaze, I encounter October's quiet, radiant beauty. In the distant wetlands, the maples are beginning to turn yellow, orange, and red, and the blue-purple asters are in bloom throughout the countryside. Our surrounding hillsides are a spectacle of rare beauty, especially at sunset.

The daily work of the harvest continues at a steady pace in our vegetable garden because any day now we may get an early frost. Today I'm harvesting our shallot and garlic bulbs for use throughout the winter. Years ago a local Italian family gave us bulbs from Tuscany, their native land. They've cultivated it with great success, and they offered me some. How could I refuse such a humble yet splendid gift? Our Tuscan garlic has yielded real wonders, and not only in our own gardens: After years of successful plantings, our original garlic bulbs have been shared with other gardeners. Today their expansion includes not only Dutchess County, but also upstate New York, New England, Pennsylvania, and New Jersey.

Garlic is a wonderful and unique gift from God. It's so in vogue that a Hudson Valley village called Saugerties has a yearly garlic festival. Thousands of people spend the day tasting garlicky products that include traditional garlic dishes such as bruschetta, vegetables, and meats prepared with garlic, and even garlic-spiked ice cream! The once-humble small garlic bulb has become a staple in most homes and a required ingredient in the kitchen of every good restaurant.

Small garlic cloves need almost a year and a half before they can be harvested. Besides good soil and weather, good garlic cultivation demands patience on the part of the grower. The ground must be carefully prepared. The cloves must be planted in rows, root side down. Some growers in the Hudson Valley prefer harvesting the bulbs a bit earlier in the season, around late July or early August, so they can cure and preserve them dry for the winter. I start harvesting as I need them in early August. If I leave them a bit longer underground, they continue to grow and they develop an even stronger flavor. They also continue to burst with that delicious fresh juice.

Consistent with the garlic treasures from the garden and the gift of fresh eggs from our own chickens, our supper tonight will consist of a basic garlic soup, German style. This means the preparation and style are different from the traditional garlic

The Provençal cook always affirms that a mortar and pestle should always smell of garlic.

PROVENÇAL SAYING

soup from the south of France. This German-style garlic recipe was shared by a dear friend who recently visited Germany. The soup will be followed by a simple buffet of fresh vegetables accompanied by the Provençal garlic mayonnaise aioli.

We serve this simple, healthy, and delicious dinner in the monastery a few times a year. We prepare it throughout the summer for informal picnics and celebrations as well as at the end of the growing season when so many fresh vegetables are at our disposal. It's a big relief for the cook when our monastic supper consists of a simple dish of fresh vegetables dipped in aioli sauce because outside of the cleaning and trimming of the vegetables, the only real work in the kitchen is the aioli preparation. Nothing could be simpler!

GARLIC CREAM SOUP (German Style)

6 SERVINGS

3 large onions, peeled and
    coarsely chopped
6 tender celery stalks, thinly sliced
2 medium garlic bulbs,
    peeled and chopped
½ stick of butter
2 cups water
2 cups milk
1 cup cream or half-and-half
Salt and white pepper

1 Sauté butter in a good-size saucepan for 3 to 4 minutes at most. Stir continuously. Add water, milk, and cream. Simmer gently over low heat for 12 to 15 minutes. Season with salt and pepper and allow to cool.

2 Purée soup in a blender or with an electric hand mixer. Reheat and serve hot.

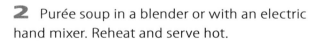

MONASTERY HARVEST SALAD WITH AIOLI SAUCE

6–8 SERVINGS

6 hard-boiled eggs,
   peeled and halved lengthwise
1 medium-size cauliflower,
   trimmed, florets separated
4 beets, washed and trimmed,
   sliced into chunks or large cubes
6 pepper tomatoes,
   quartered lengthwise
1 avocado, peeled, quartered
   lengthwise and then halved
12 fresh radishes, trimmed
2 medium-size cucumbers,
   peeled and cut into large cubes
12 pitted black olives

AIOLI SAUCE

2 very fresh egg yolks
4 garlic cloves, minced
1 tablespoon fresh lemon juice or
   tarragon vinegar
1 teaspoon Dijon mustard
Salt and white pepper
1 cup light olive oil or vegetable oil

1 Prepare aioli sauce on the day you plan to serve it. In a deep bowl, combine egg yolks, lemon juice, and mustard and season with salt and pepper. Mix with a whisk or electric mixer until uniform and creamy.

2 Add 1 teaspoon of oil at a time, whisking or mixing until aioli thickens. Add garlic. Mix until consistency is even. Refrigerate for a few hours before serving.

3 Boil cauliflower florets in salted water for exactly 3 minutes. Drain under cold water and set aside. In a separate pan, boil beets in salted water for 3 minutes. Drain under cold water and set aside.

4 Place the bowl the aioli will be served in at the center of a large platter. Around the bowl, assemble hard-boiled eggs and vegetables in groups. Fill the bowl with aioli, and serve immediately.

NOTE: TO EAT THIS DISH IN TRUE PROVENÇAL STYLE, THE PLATTER SHOULD BE AT THE CENTER OF THE TABLE, WITH SMALL PLATES FOR EACH PERSON TO SELF SERVE. SERVE PLENTY OF FRESH FRENCH BREAD TO CLEAN UP THE DELICIOUS AIOLI LEFT ON THE PLATES.

LATE SEPTEMBER–early October is the extraordinary time of year when summer almost imperceptibly blends into autumn. The fields of fresh green corn have been replaced with tons of red and orange pumpkins. Local farmers are almost delirious with what seems to be a prolific harvest as they proudly continue to show their wares at the road stands. Those road stands, a counterpart to the weekly farmers' market, are rich in harvest goods. In addition to the newly picked pumpkins and squash, you see apples of all varieties, pears, new potatoes, onions, garlic, tomatoes, beets, Swiss chard, peppers, eggplants, cabbages, and all the late vegetables as well as ravishing bouquets of zinnias and sunflowers, to say nothing of the newly arrived chrysanthemums in fall colors. Some stands also offer fresh cider pressed right there on the spot or brought from one of the local presses.

Today was long and arduous. It's very likely that tonight we'll have a real frost. I say *real* because we had a mild frost a few days ago that didn't do too much damage. I covered the basil and the most fragile plants, and they survived well. I don't know what the outcome of tonight's frost will be, so besides the garlic, shallots, and other vegetables I'm harvesting today, I'm also bringing in the last of the eggplants, hot peppers, pole beans, beets, and lots (but not all) of the almost-ripe tomatoes.

As I bring in the baskets of tomatoes and other goods, I notice today's glorious sunset. The sun's last rays, flickering and radiant, convey a very nostalgic feeling. I become deeply aware that the long hours of summer sun are gone and the countdown to winter has begun. As I take a final glance outdoors, I see the long line of trees standing tall and silent, as if in awe, before the quiet majesty of today's sunset. Both the trees and the chilly air have their own way of saying goodbye to the day and greeting evening's arrival with anticipation.

As I proceed into the kitchen with baskets laden with harvest goods, I take a few moments to rest and be still. Stillness is a way of recollecting, of remaining silent, of understanding at a deeper level what is happening in the moment. Stillness allows me to unravel the mystery that was today: the magical hours of another fall day, even if they were tiring. Being still also permits me to remain centered as I taste the monastic peace, one of God's greatest gifts to us in this monastery, and give thanks for the grace of the moment.

The shallot is often an important ingredient in my cooking. I appreciate its special mild flavor. Garlic and onions are too strong for some dishes, and a good shallot is a fine substitute. Having grown up in the Pyrenees, where the traditional shallot was

*Lord, I do fear
Thou'st made
the world too
beautiful this year;
My soul is all but
out of me—let fall
No burning leaf;
prithee let no
bird call.*

EDNA ST. VINCENT MILLAY

always handy, I needed no extra encouragement to cultivate these aromatic bulbs in our monastery garden.

About ten years ago I brought some shallot bulbs from Valence and started experimenting with its cultivation here. At the end of the first harvest, fifty bulbs had multiplied into well over three hundred. I used about two thirds of that harvest saved about one third for the next planting. This system has worked well for us: Each year we harvest more than enough to share with friends and neighbors.

The shallots harvested today will be placed in our dry cellar, arranged tomorrow over newspapers, and dried for ten to twelve days. When they're dry, I'll gently break the bulbs apart and place them in small wooden baskets to stash for winter use. It's important to keep them in a safe, dry place. Later these shallots will enrich our soups, salads, and sauces with subtle, sweet flavor. I especially enjoy them as a substitute for onions in a raw salad or warm potato salad. I also like to chop and mince a shallot bulb, place it in an expeditiously made vinaigrette, and let it stand for a few hours before mixing it with a salad.

Shallots can also enhance beets or string beans, as in tonight's appetizer. Their sweet, unobtrusive taste combines very well with these vegetables. It's a welcome change from the typical use of onions on such occasions.

BEETS IN CREAMY SHALLOT VINAIGRETTE   6 SERVINGS

8 medium-size fresh red beets, washed, peeled, and cut into cubes or matchsticks
¼ cup fresh lemon juice
1 head of fresh lettuce

SHALLOT VINAIGRETTE
2 tablespoons tarragon-scented wine vinegar
8 tablespoons extra-virgin olive oil
1 teaspoon Dijon mustard
Salt and freshly ground pepper
4 tablespoons heavy cream
2 medium-size shallots, coarsely chopped and then minced
A few fresh parsley sprigs, finely chopped

1 Cook beets in a large saucepan of boiling salted water for about 5 minutes or until tender. Drain, rinse under cold running water, and drain again thoroughly. Place beets in a deep bowl, add lemon juice, mix well, and refrigerate for at least 2 hours.

2 Prepare vinaigrette by whirling in a blender vinegar, olive oil, mustard, and salt and pepper. Add cream and whirl again until the mixture turns into a smooth sauce. Just before serving, add shallots. Mix well with a fork or spoon. Pour sauce over beets. Mix well.

3 Prepare a bed of lettuce (3 or 4 leaves) on each serving plate. Spoon beets onto the center of the lettuce. Garnish with finely chopped parsley. Serve cold.

ALMOST SUDDENLY, over the last few days autumn's glorious splendor has peaked. Here in the Northeast, the foliage always seems at its best around the Columbus Day weekend. Hordes of tourists drop in on the local countryside, roaming around, seeking the best vistas for their cameras, and taking rides to the farms and vineyards and the picturesque villages of Rhinebeck, Millbrook, Kent, and Salisbury. On these fall days everything seems brighter and more intimate. We face the zenith and decline of a beautiful season and get ready for winter. Temperatures will begin to fall, daylight will recede, and early darkness will envelop us. As we head into the monastic chapel around 5:30 PM to sing Vespers, it will no longer be daylight. The incomparable glow of the sun's dying rays will bestow quiet, peace, and reassurance as we intone our eventide praise to the Lord.

On this bright autumn morning I had unexpected visitors, a couple from Long Island. They wanted to buy our monastery vinegar, which we produce the old-fashioned, artisanal way. I asked what brought them to this part of the country and the young woman immediately replied, "The scenery at this time of year, in this part of the country, is spectacular." "Yes," I said, "Dutchess County, Ulster, Columbia, and Litchfield especially offer some of the most evocative sights. The fiery red maples, the yellow and gold of the aspens, the bronze from the oak and birch trees—they all mix with the pines and other evergreens to create a true tapestry of colors. Nothing really surpasses them!"

I showed them our garden's abundance of unharvested tomatoes, peppers, and eggplants. Pointing out the crop of Japanese eggplants, I told them the first thing that had come to mind for tonight's supper was a large pot of good Provençal Ratatouille.

Ratatouille is probably one of the better-known Provençal vegetable dishes. It's also one of the more misunderstood and consequently is often poorly made. A good ratatouille demands long preparation, and it's not as simple as many suppose. Often the eggplants and zucchini must be prepared ahead, first by salting them and allowing them to sweat, to use an old French expression. This technique is often ignored by incompetent cooks, and the result is a poorly made ratatouille.

The name *ratatouille* comes from the French word *touiller*, "to stir up," which is how ratatouille is prepared. It requires stirring for several hours, and thus very patient arms and hands.

May those who sow in tears reap with shouts of joy.

PSALM 126:5

There are as many ratatouille recipes as there are cooks in Provence. Each claims to have his or her own secret, from the number of vegetables used to the use or absence of certain herbs from Provence. In my view, there are certain essentials, such as the preparation of the vegetables and the stirring. The rest, I think, can be accommodated to whatever works best for each chef.

Here is our basic recipe, straight from Provence, as I once learned to prepare it guided by the gentle hand and advice of a dutiful Provençal friend.

RATATOUILLE A LA PROVENÇAL

6–8 SERVINGS

1 pound Japanese eggplants, sliced
Sea salt
Virgin olive oil
1 pound zucchini, cut in slices
1 red pepper, thinly sliced
1 yellow pepper, thinly sliced
1 green pepper, thinly sliced
2 medium-to-large Vidalia onions, chopped
10 plum tomatoes, peeled, seeded, and coarsely chopped
6 garlic cloves, peeled and minced
2 teaspoons sugar
1 bay leaf
Handful of basil leaves and thyme sprigs, chopped
Handful of large Italian-type parsley, chopped
Freshly ground pepper

1 Place eggplants on a large platter, sprinkle with salt, and let stand for at least 1 hour.

2 Pour about 10 tablespoons of olive oil (more if needed) into a large frying pan or saucepan. Drain eggplants and add to them to the pan. Brown on both sides over medium heat. Remove and drain with paper towels. Add a bit more oil to the pan and cook zucchini the same way. Remove and drain. Cook peppers the same way for a short while. Remove and drain.

3 Add a bit more oil to the pan and cook onions until soft but not brown. Add tomatoes, garlic, sugar, basil, thyme, parsley, and pepper. Simmer for about 30 minutes, stirring from time to time. Add remaining vegetables and stir 5 to 10 minutes. Taste and check seasonings. Remove bay leaf. Serve ratatouille warm or lukewarm. During the summer, refrigerate and serve cold.

THE WEATHER continues to change. Bright, sunny days alternate with rainy, chilly days on which the drift from the winds is felt to the bones. Today is one of those days, so the first thing I did this morning was light the wood-burning stove in the east corner of the kitchen. Our five cats, Misty, Ebony, Fluffy, Nicole, and Margot, love that spot. During the cold winter nights they sleep close by the stove, the five of them together without any fights.

I relish the moment I step indoors, where the wood stove's welcoming warmth and sweet fragrance greet and comfort us. The scent of the burning wood is almost intoxicating, sweet as a good dream, I often say. Today is that way. It's not made for outdoor work. I'll spend the day making our artisanal vinegars for the local vineyard, for a restaurant in New York City, for friends of the monastery, and for our Christmas sale. The grapes take about three months to ferment into good-quality vinegar, so I'm running a bit late for the Christmas stock. The Millbrook vineyard sells our vinegar locally and through a catalog. They offer it in a lovely Christmas basket with their excellent olive oil, which is produced on their own Tuscany property in Italy.

One reason I enjoy working in the comfort of our kitchen is that I can listen to beautiful music while I work. Good music doesn't interrupt monastic silence—it enhances it. Many monasteries in Europe listen to music as the monks, nuns, and their guests eat. The music is heard in silence, and sometimes during those precious moments one can almost feel the intensity of that silence.

Today is the Feast of Saint Luke, one of the four evangelists. I like to think about Saint Luke, of whose Gospel I am particularly fond, while listening to Chopin's "Cello Sonata in G Minor." It's jewel of a piece, written with the maturity that comes only at the end of one's life. I'm particularly attracted to the cello parts of the sonata, where an outpouring of ravishing melodies seems to sing with a poignancy the cello alone can convey. I find the cello almost irreplaceable. The recording I'm enjoying this morning is by the cellist Jacqueline du Pré who, like Chopin, tragically died young. Something of Chopin's story exists in her story, in her art, in her music-making.

As I work, I realize the menu for tonight's meal must be considered rather quickly. With the multiple tasks in the kitchen, including bringing in wood from the outside and tending to the stove, there isn't time for lengthy food preparation. On such occasions I rely on pasta dishes or quick omelettes.

A good friend from New York City recently brought us a box of figs, of which I'm

*Once I knew
a kitchen where
the woodsmoke
smelled so sweet,
Excited sparks flew
out the drafts
and glowing,
cheery heat
Filled the homey
room with joy
beyond all
modern measure.*

RUTH B. FIELD

extremely fond. I usually don't use them here in our cooking because they're beyond the cost level of what one usually spends in a monastery. We try to live our values of simplicity, moderation, and frugality in all things. But who can refuse a gift?

Since figs are healthful, nutritious, easy to digest, low in fat, and high in fiber, I designed a recipe that needs only a bit of cheese and nuts to complete it. Served with a green salad and a baked apple, this dish is all we need to sustain and comfort our tired bodies. The chill in the air calls for comfort food, and this meal should certainly do that for us.

PASTA WITH FIGS AND CHEDDAR CHEESE

4–6 SERVINGS

4 teaspoons olive oil

⅓ cup pine nuts

1½ cups heavy cream or half-and-half

¾ cup New York State or Vermont cheddar cheese, cut into very small pieces

½ cup Parmesan cheese, grated

A few sprigs of fresh parsley or chervil, finely chopped

1½ pounds fettuccine or other pasta

10 fresh figs, sliced into wedges; use dry figs if fresh aren't available

Salt and freshly ground pepper

1 Pour olive oil into a skillet, add pine nuts, and stir over low–medium heat for 2 to 3 minutes. Set aside.

2 Pour cream into a saucepan, add cheese and parsley (or chervil), and continue stirring over low–medium heat until cheese melts into a thick sauce.

3 In another pan as sauce cooks, prepare pasta according to package instructions until *al dente*. Drain pasta, add pine nuts and figs, and pour sauce over pasta. Sprinkle with freshly ground pepper. Mix well and serve hot. Top with extra Parmesan cheese or serve the cheese in a bowl so each person may add it to taste.

THE FOLIAGE COLORS are proceeding rapidly toward their decline. They peaked in mid October, and the bright colors lasted until now. But with the heavy rains and winds of the last few days, the trees are rapidly losing their leaves. After sunset, the nights are getting colder and longer. Soon our clocks will be returning to Eastern Standard Time, and the somber night hours will be prolonged.

All these signals foretell the coming winter. The autumn season is well underway and the multiple winter preparations continue in the monastery, but the harvest work cannot be totally ignored. This has been a very good year for apples and other fruits in the Hudson Valley. Since several local growers kindly suggest to us we pick the remaining apples on the ground before the deer get to them or they're destroyed by heavy frosts, I decide to take another trip to the orchards.

It's always a refreshing experience and joyful occasion when I have a chance to head north to visit these local orchards and gather the last of the apples. Apples, of course, are used in a myriad of ways in the monastery, not only for dessert but also for apple butter, jelly, and jam. I also mix apples in salads with cooked squash, sweet potatoes, greens, endives, or beets.

I never cease giving thanks to the Lord for allowing me to share the life of this rich agricultural region of New York State, the Hudson Valley, where all kinds of fruits are cultivated on both sides of the river: apples, pears, peaches, berries, and plums, not to mention the glorious grapes used to produce renowned wines from the Valley and from which our own vinegar is made.

I collect six bushels of apples. Some apples are a bit touched and must be consumed quickly. The rest are in good shape and will last in our cellar for a while. I'm a bit exhausted, plus Vespers must be sung before the meals. I quickly decide to prepare a plate of scrambled eggs with plenty of fresh parsley and a baked dish that combines apples and recently harvested squash. Simple and quick, this dish will be in the oven while Vespers is celebrated in the chapel. By doing this, I save a half hour of cooking time. A simple but delicious apple dessert will complete the meal.

You cannot hope to enjoy the harvest without first laboring in the field.

AUTHOR UNKNOWN

BAKED BUTTERNUT SQUASH AND APPLES

6–8 SERVINGS

2 butternut squash, peeled, seeded, and cubed
5 apples, peeled, thinly sliced
2 teaspoons lemon juice
½ cup brown sugar
Dash of cinnamon
4 tablespoons butter
½ cup cider or apple juice
3 tablespoons raisins

1 Cook squash in salted boiling water 12 to 15 minutes or until done. Drain and set aside.

2 Place apples in boiling water, add lemon juice, and cook 4 to 5 minutes. Drain and save water to use in place of cider or apple juice if they're not available. (I often do this with vegetable or fruit juices.)

3 Preheat oven to 350° F. Place squash and apples in a large bowl. Mash and blend well. Add sugar, cinnamon, butter, apple juice or water, and raisins. Mix well.

4 Thoroughly butter a good-size elongated baking dish and fill it with the squash-apple mixture. Even out the top with a spatula. Sprinkle brown sugar over the top and dot here and there with butter. Bake for 30 minutes. Serve hot.

APPLES ON CALVADOS NORMANDY STYLE

6–8 SERVINGS

5 large tart apples, peeled
3 tablespoons sweet butter
½ cup calvados liqueur
½ cup sugar
1 teaspoon vanilla extract
Vanilla ice cream

1 Use a melon baller to cut apples into small or medium balls.

2 Heat butter in a large skillet, add calvados, sugar, and vanilla extract and stir well over low-medium heat for 1 or 2 minutes. Add apple balls. Stir and shake skillet frequently for 3 to 4 minutes or until apples are cooked and tender. Add more calvados if needed. Top with vanilla ice cream and serve immediately.

WHEN THE FOLIAGE peaks with bright oranges, scarlet reds, and golden yellows, you can see that autumn stands on its own ground, that it's distinctly different from the other seasons with its own glamor and beauty. Often, as I pause to savor the loveliness of the season, I notice how much autumn is a time of transition. Gone is the lushness, the exuberance and the excitement of the summer days. By now, in the natural flow of time, those days have merged into the more reflective mood of the rapidly approaching winter. Soon it will be November and the Feast of All Saints. The cool air will invigorate during the day; at night, however, the longer hours will turn chilly and damp, and dusk will descend upon us at a moment's notice.

The physical work outdoors, which consists mostly of preparations for winter, continues at a steady pace. Today we planted tulip bulbs for next spring and gathered the last herbs from the garden, including plenty of mint in all varieties, lemon verbena, parsley, chervil, thyme, oregano, chives, and other collectibles. They won't last if left outdoors, so they must be picked quickly.

Other jobs include raking the leaves, cleaning the yard, hauling and stacking firewood, trimming the last perennials to bloom, and properly cleaning and storing the garden tools. There is so much to do and so little time. Yet every year at this time, the story is repeated.

No one doubts the amount of physical work the maintenance of a monastic property entails. As stewards of the land, monks have upheld these traditions for centuries, and they will continue to do so as long as monasteries survive. As Psalm 107:37–38 aptly describes,

> *They sow fields, and plant vineyards,*
> *and get a fruitful yield.*
> *By his blessing they multiply greatly,*
> *and he does not let their cattle decrease.*

Because we have so many apples at this time, they become the *de rigueur* daily staple in our meals. These fresh, local apples have a distinct flavor I've grown accustomed to.

In preparing desserts made with apples, I like to alternate new, innovative recipes with more traditional, old-fashioned ones. I look for new recipes in food magazines

Let them thank the Lord for his steadfast love, for his wonderful works to humankind. For he satisfies the thirsty, and the hungry he fills with good things.

PSALM 107:8–9

and the local paper and search for old recipes in old cookbooks and from friends here and in France. I change them a bit, adding or subtracting according to taste, impulse, or ingredient availability. The outcome is usually good and refreshingly new.

In all cases, I try to hold on to the principles of simplicity and restraint, a must in all monastic and French traditional cooking. Ideally, the result is light, appetizing, elegant in its simplicity and, of course, nourishing.

Tonight's dessert is an old-fashioned recipe from a friend from Minnesota. It's basic and simple.

APPLE DUMPLINGS GERMAN STYLE

6 SERVINGS

2 cups flour
2 teaspoons baking powder
½ teaspoon salt
⅔ cup shortening
½ cup milk
7 tart apples, peeled
½ teaspoon cinnamon
Dash of nutmeg
¾ cup brown sugar
6 tablespoons butter
½ cup brown sugar
½ cup white sugar
2 cups water
2 tablespoons calvados liqueur
(optional)
6 tablespoons butter

1 In a deep bowl mix and sift the flour, baking powder, salt, and shortening. Work mixture lightly with your fingertips.

2 Make a hole in the mixture's center and gradually add milk. Stir and mix. Knead lightly into a ball, then roll into a rectangular-shaped piece of dough about ¼-inch thick. Cut dough into 6 pieces.

3 Slice apples and divide among the six squares of dough. Mix cinnamon, nutmeg, and brown sugar. Add to apples.

4 Dot each square with 1 tablespoon of butter. Gather corners of each piece of dough. Pinch corners together to form a dumpling.

5 Preheat oven to 350° F. Mix brown sugar, white sugar, water, calvados, and butter to make a syrup over low-medium heat. Mix and blend well. Butter a long baking dish. Carefully place dumplings in it, pour syrup evenly over the top, and bake for 45 minutes to 1 hour or until dumplings are done. Serve hot.

NOVEMBER

*Now the bonfires
flicker softly in the
glow of eventide,
and the cooling
breath of autumn
stirs in the heart,
while deep inside
there's a vivid
lasting picture
painted with
a brush divine
of a country town
in autumn
and November
days that shine!*

FLORENCE DELONG

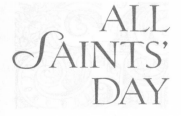

ALL
SAINTS'
DAY

NOVEMBER IS A UNIQUE MONTH in the kitchen calendar. It's the month of All Saints, All Souls, Saint Martin of Tours, and, of course, Thanksgiving, which occurs when harvest labors are almost over. It's the time we celebrate God's blessings upon a good harvest, the products of the bounty of our gardens, fields, and orchards, just before winter sets in.

When I think about the food most appropriate for November celebrations or for ordinary meals on gray November days, I think of pumpkins and squash freshly harvested from our fields. The *curcurbita maxima,* as a large squash is called in Latin, is more popular than any other vegetable at this time of year. In the Mediterranean world, the humble *potiron,* as squash is called in France, occupies a singular place in the daily winter fare of monasteries, homes, and even fancy restaurants.

From antiquity on, the European-Mediterranean countries always held the ever-eclectic squash in high esteem. It was as deeply appreciated by the early inhabitants of the Americas. Research has shown that the squash was a daily staple in the Andean countries, particularly Peru, Chile, and Bolivia.

One of my favorite November recipes is what we call in French *crème de potiron,* creamy pumpkin soup. This recipe fares better when using the French type of pumpkin, which has more taste than the regular American variety used for decoration. Thank God the French variety is now cultivated here and can be easily found in American markets. I always manage to bring seeds from France and then grow them in our monastic garden. The gentle sweet flavor of the soup is enhanced by the use of *crème fraîche* ("fresh cream," cream that has been made thicker with lactic acid) and the béchamel sauce that transforms it into an experience of pure delight.

As we celebrate the great Solemnity of All Saints, I make use of the newly harvested pumpkins. This solemnity recalls the deep mystery of the communion of saints. Therefore, it is the celebration of the large multitude around God's throne and of God's family in which all his children take part. I am filled with joy as I work in the kitchen, feeling close to all God's children, those often remembered and those long forgotten. Today they come together and somehow become visible in my mind as I unite myself with them in the worship and adoration of God.

One of the many uses of pumpkin in the monastery is creating our own unique pumpkin-vanilla jam, which always turns out delicious. I enhance our recipe, originally from France, with whatever spices are available. Orange juice adds a lovely sweet-tart flavor to the jam.

CRÈME DE POTIRON (Creamy Pumpkin Soup)

6–8 SERVINGS

10–12 cups water

1 medium-size French pumpkin, peeled and diced

4 leeks, sliced (white parts only)

5 medium-size potatoes, peeled and diced

Salt

5 tablespoons virgin olive oil

6 tablespoons crème fraîche or low-fat sour cream

2 eggs, well beaten

A few sprigs of parsley, finely chopped

BÉCHAMEL SAUCE

3 tablespoons butter

2 tablespoons cornstarch

1½ cups milk

Nutmeg

White pepper

1 Pour water into large soup kettle. Add pumpkin, leeks, potatoes, and salt. Bring water to a boil, then lower heat to medium. Cook for about 30 minutes.

2 Turn off heat and allow soup to cool. Whirl soup in a blender and then reheat gradually over low to medium heat. Add olive oil and crème fraîche or sour cream. Stir well.

3 Make a quick béchamel sauce by melting butter in a stainless steel pan over medium heat. Add cornstarch, stirring continuously. Gradually add milk as you continue stirring. Add salt, white pepper, and nutmeg to taste and continue stirring. When sauce begins to boil, reduce heat to low and continue stirring until sauce thickens.

4 Add béchamel sauce to soup and stir well. Beat eggs thoroughly and add to soup. Mix well. Check seasonings and add more salt or pepper if needed.

5 Continue to cook and stir soup for another 20 minutes. Serve hot topped with finely chopped parsley.

PUMPKIN JAM

10 OR 12 8-OUNCE JARS

1 bottle Marsala wine

½ gallon orange juice

1 good-size pumpkin or hubbard (winter) squash, peeled, seeded, and diced

1 vanilla bean

10 apples (or pears), peeled, seeded, and cut into thin slices

1 cinnamon stick

4 cups brown or white sugar

1¾-ounce package of pectin

1 Place ingredients in a large pot and bring to a boil. Boil about 30 minutes or until mushy. Reduce heat to medium. Continue cooking and stirring with a large, long wooden spoon. Cook until mixture gels (test a sample on a chilled saucer; it should harden after a few minutes).

2 Mixture is ready when it hardens. Pour jam in sterilized jars, put lids on jars, and place them in a large pan of boiling water. Allow water to boil for 20 to 30 minutes or until jars seal properly. Carefully withdraw jars from water and allow them to cool for 24 hours before storing.

HEAVY RAINS have shaken the leaves from our trees, leaving them almost totally bare. The glorious fall colors that have until recently graced our New York–New England landscape are gently leaving us until next year. The chilly November days are here.

I'm spending the afternoon in the kitchen planning the evening meal as I listen to Beethoven's Quartet Op. 74, No. 10. This sort of music enhances the human spirit no matter what state of mind we find ourselves in or whatever weather we are enduring. Listening to Beethoven allows me to find the quiet pulse of our monastic kitchen on this chilly November day. The quartet and the silence capture a feeling of simple contentment, calm, and inner peace. The music centers me as I labor steadily, cleaning both the kitchen and the refrigerator, before I immerse myself in the details of the evening repast.

After looking through my repertoire of fall recipes and checking the ingredients readily available for tonight's simple supper, I decide to make *lasagnes au potiron*, baked lasagna with cooked mashed pumpkin. Following the irresistible lasagna, I'll serve a simple salad with an aged cheese whose overtones and intense taste enrich the character of any homemade meal. A succulent hot lasagna dish and a salad bowl of crisp, fresh greens are all one needs on a cool November night.

I wish I could say our salad-and-cheese course would be accompanied by a good muscat wine like Beaumes-de-Venise, as is often done in Provence. Reality tells me that a plain upstate New York monastery must be content with a simple full-bodied ordinary wine. May God be praised in all things!

No sun—

no moon!

No morn!

No noon.

No shade,

no shine,

no butterflies,

no bees,

No fruits,

no flowers,

no leaves,

no birds,

November!

THOMAS HOOD

LASAGNES AU POTIRON (Pumpkin Lasagna)

6 SERVINGS

1 medium-size pumpkin, French or
   American, peeled and cubed
1 teaspoon nutmeg
1½ pounds spinach or Swiss chard,
   coarsely chopped
¼ cup golden raisins, finely chopped
1 large-size onion, coarsely chopped
2 hard-boiled eggs, coarsely chopped
2 garlic cloves, finely chopped
Pepper
1 egg
1 quart low-fat ricotta cheese
3 teaspoons fresh thyme (or dried)
Salt and pepper
12 lasagna noodles
1 tablespoon olive oil
4 cups tomato sauce,
   preferably homemade
Butter

1 Boil pumpkin cubes in salted water 10 to 15 minutes. Drain completely and place back in the empty pot. Add nutmeg and mash coarsely. Mix well and set aside.

2 Boil spinach or Swiss chard in salted water for 15 minutes or until tender. Drain completely and place back in the empty pot. Add golden raisins, chopped onion, chopped eggs, chopped garlic, and freshly ground pepper to taste. Mix well.

3 Preheat oven to 350° F.

4 Beat 1 egg in a deep bowl, add ricotta, thyme, and a dash of salt and pepper. Mix well and set aside.

5 Boil lasagna noodles in a large container. Add olive oil and a dash of salt. Cook for 5 minutes. Pasta must remain *al dente*. Drain.

6 Butter or oil a 9-inch by 9-inch ovenproof lasagna dish. Pour tomato sauce in the bottom of the dish and spread evenly with a spatula. Place 4 lasagna noodles over sauce. Top noodles with a thin layer of mashed pumpkin. Place another layer of noodles on top. Top noodles with a thin layer of spinach-egg mixture. Top spinach with a thin layer of ricotta mixture. Top ricotta mixture with 4 more lasagna noodles and 1 cup tomato sauce. Repeat entire procedure, ending with a layer of lasagna noodles topped with 1 cup tomato sauce. Cover with foil and bake 35 to 40 minutes. Remove foil and bake for 10 minutes. Remove from oven and serve hot.

FRENCH CHEFS are often reproached for using copious amounts of butter, cream, milk, and cheese to achieve flavorful results. Those who criticize French traditional cooking methods say French chefs will resort to anything, healthy or not, to make food taste good.

There may be a certain truth to the concerns about the use of butter, cream, and cheese in traditional French cooking, but I don't think it's as bad now as it used to be. A great chef, French or otherwise, can achieve superb results without totally relying on fats or similar staples. Today's great French chefs are innovative and have learned to improve on traditional French cooking by making use of healthier ingredients. In my own cooking, I follow Saint Benedict's timeless advice and wisdom: "Moderation in all things." This counsel has helped me create recipes compatible with our monastic life and that illustrate its innate simplicity, purity, and frugality.

Tonight's meal continues the theme of squash and pumpkins. The main course for our frugal monastic meal is a dish called *polenta et zucca*, inspired by the cooking of the Piedmont in Italy. It's just the right dish to prove that a congenial and appetizing meal can be prepared without fattening ingredients. The small amount of cheese adds protein to create a balanced meal. Accompanied by a good green salad, this succulent dish is a perfect meal for a chilly November evening.

Lucca mihi
patria est.
*The squash is
my homeland.*

TEOFILO FOLENGO

POLENTA E ZUCCA (Polenta With Squash)

6–8 SERVINGS

8 cups water, more if needed
2 butternut squash, peeled,
    seeded, and cubed
Pinch of salt
7 cups water
2 cups coarse cornmeal
Salt
Freshly ground pepper
1 small onion, finely chopped
½ teaspoon dried rosemary
½ teaspoon dried sage
4 tablespoons olive oil
Grated Parmesan cheese
Olive oil

1 Bring water to a boil in a large pot. Add squash cubes and a pinch of salt and boil for about 20 minutes. Drain and purée squash with a masher. Set aside.

2 Bring water to a boil in a large pot. lowly pour in cornmeal in small quantities. Stir constantly to prevent lumps. Add salt and pepper to taste and continue stirring until mixture acquires an even, thick consistency. Add chopped onion, rosemary, sage, and olive oil. Mix well and remove from heat.

3 Preheat oven to 350° F.

4 Add squash purée and about 6 tablespoons of grated Parmesan cheese to polenta. Mix thoroughly.

5 Oil a long, rectangular baking dish. Spread squash and polenta mixture evenly. Sprinkle with grated Parmesan cheese. Bake for 30 to 40 minutes. Remove from oven and let cool a few minutes before serving hot.

TODAY there is great joy in the monastery as we celebrate the memorial of a truly monastic saint, Martin of Tours. Here in our small monastic enclave, his memorial is a ray of sunlight in the midst of our somber and sometimes bleak November. Saint Martin's life and example have deeply influenced my own monastic life, so I regard him with great affection and gratitude. Today I am reminded once more that before anything else, he was a monk through and through.

The day's expressive joy is palpable, especially in the liturgical offices and the kitchen. In contrast to our everyday monastic sobriety, Saint Martin's Day is an occasion for a festive and restorative evening meal—one following our French tradition, because Saint Martin is one of France's patron saints.

After the morning Office, singing Saint Martin's praises, I plan our principal meal of the day. I always enjoy mentally running through the possibilities for the evening meal. Because tonight's meal is special, I have anticipated for days what the main course will be: a timeless, basic soufflé I make only a few times a year. Today's soup, a seasonal one, is *potage de citrouille*, a rare soup that combines the marvelous

Filled with joy, Martin was welcomed by Abraham. Martin left this life a poor and lowly man and entered heaven rich in God's favor.

LAUDS ANTIPHONE
OF THE FEAST

flavors of squash, leeks, and celery root. It's a quintessential soup from the Midi, as the south of France is called. After the soup and soufflé, a simple fresh green salad and a dessert of *pears au vin* will complete the festive menu.

I'm particularly fond of this soup, a rather typical November–December dish in which the rustic and elegant ingredients commingle perfectly to achieve a most appetizing result. The subtle taste of the celery root accentuates the soup and almost gives it a hint of luxury. It's a pity we don't grow celery root in our garden, since it's rather expensive and rare in the supermarkets.

POTAGE DE CITROUILLE (Squash, Leek, and Celery-Root Soup)
6–8 SERVINGS

1 medium-size hubbard (winter)
   squash (or pumpkin),
   peeled and diced
1 large celery root, trimmed,
   peeled, and cubed
3 medium-size potatoes,
   peeled and diced
3 leeks, thinly sliced
   (white parts only)
12 cups water
Salt and freshly ground pepper
1 cup heavy cream
   (or 1 small container of low-fat
   sour cream, about a quart)
Fresh chervil

1 Combine vegetables in a good-size soup pot. Add water and bring it to a quick boil. Lower heat to medium. Add salt and pepper and cook 50 to 60 minutes without covering the pot. Add water if needed.

2 Allow soup to cool, then whirl it in the blender. Return soup to the pot and reheat it at low–medium.

3 Add heavy cream (or low-fat sour cream) and continue stirring for 15 minutes or until ingredients are equally mixed. Serve immediately in soup plates. Top with finely chopped fresh chervil (or parsley or chives if chervil isn't available).

NOTE: THIS SOUP MUST ALWAYS BE SERVED HOT.

SLOWLY BUT SURELY we're witnessing the completion of the year. Another summer has passed, and another harvest moon has reflected its magic on our fields and trees, giving us a hint of the approaching winter. This morning we awakened to one of those November days in which the chill penetrates your very bones. It feels good to work close by the warmth of the wood stove.

As I reflect on the realities the month, the day, and the weather bring, I gather strength and inspiration from the passage of 1 Peter read today at one of our monastic Offices. Indeed, God loves all his children. What is there to fear when we know this? Only through faith and deep prayer are we given the grace to personally and palpably experience his tender care for each of us.

"God opposes the proud, but gives grace to the humble."
Humble yourselves therefore under the mighty hand of God, so that he may exalt you in due time. Cast all your anxiety on him, because he cares for you.

1 PETER 5:5–7

I continue planning tonight's dinner around pumpkins and squash, God's gifts to the season and, in turn, the season's gift to us. I'm mostly inspired by seasonal produce when I assemble the daily meal. Today I've decided to make *timbale de potiron*, a dish well known and rather common at this time of the year in French monasteries. It's simple, nutritious, and easy to assemble. It also gives me the chance to use those gorgeous hubbard (winter) squash I'm so fond of.

TIMBALE DE POTIRON (Hubbard-Squash Timbale)

**1 medium-size hubbard (winter)
squash, peeled, seeded, and
cut into small chunks**
Salt
**3 eggs separated, both the yolks
and whites beaten stiff**
**1 cup grated Gruyère or
other cheese**

BÉCHAMEL SAUCE
4 tablespoons butter
3 tablespoons cornstarch
2 cups milk
Freshly ground pepper
Nutmeg

1 Place squash chunks in a large cooking pot filled with enough water to cover them. Add salt to taste and boil over medium–high heat at least 20 minutes. Drain thoroughly and place squash back into the pot. Mash it thoroughly and set aside.

2 Make a quick béchamel sauce by melting butter in a stainless steel pan over medium heat. Add cornstarch to milk. Gradually add cornstarch mixture to melted butter and continue stirring. Add salt, freshly ground pepper, and nutmeg to taste. Continue stirring. When sauce begins to boil, reduce to low–medium heat and continue stirring until sauce thickens.

3 Preheat oven to 350° F. Add béchamel sauce to mashed squash and mix well. Add beaten egg yolks and mix thoroughly. Add ½ cup grated cheese and mix.

4 Butter an elongated ovenproof dish and pour squash mixture into it. Distribute evenly. Place stiff egg whites on top of mixture. Go around dish with a small knife, making small indentations into the mixture (as in a soufflé). Gently sprinkle remaining cheese on top and place dish in oven for 30 to 35 minutes. Cool 3 minutes, then serve.

NOVEMBER'S DAMPNESS makes it seem cooler than the outdoor thermometer says it is. A deep, misty stillness hovers over the property. Winter, though still almost five weeks away, seems very close.

Putting together a good menu is always a challenge. I try to remember yesterday's main course so I don't repeat it. If there are quite a few leftovers, I save them for another time. With a bit of monastic ingenuity, I can convert them into a seemingly different dish, as is often done in France. *L'art d'utilizer les restes,* the French call it: "The art of reusing leftovers."

Sometimes I struggle between preparing something quick and easy and something a bit more elaborate. I calculate the amount of time allocated within the monastic schedule for cooking and the time of preparation a certain dish requires. The wisdom is in knowing the difference and finding a close balance between the two.

I begin planning our meals by finding out what is available in the kitchen, garden, and cellar. We always start with a soup, except in the summer when have a simple appetizer such as fresh tomatoes in olive oil or beets remoulade. A dish of fresh green salad follows. Dessert will most likely be fresh fruit or fruit compote.

Look to this day!
For it is life,
the very life of life.
In its brief course
lie all the verities
and realities
of existence:
The bliss of growth,
The glory of action,
The splendor
of achievement.

KALIDASA

As most people who have visited French monasteries know, compote is a traditional part of the daily fare. On a feast day or solemnity, we may celebrate and indulge in a better and more elaborate homemade dessert, and that is just how it should be. Church and monastic feast days are not relegated solely to the chapel and its liturgical expressions: often they find their most human expression in the sacrament at the table in the agape.

Tonight's main course, risotto with butternut squash, continues our squash theme. Risotto is always a most welcome dish, particularly during the cold months.

RISOTTO AU POTIRON (Risotto With Butternut Squash)

4–6 SERVINGS

4 tablespoons butter

2 medium-size onions,
   chopped and minced

1 medium-size butternut squash,
   peeled, seeded, and cubed

2 cups arborio rice

5 mushrooms, cleaned and
   sliced thinly

5 cups boiling water or chicken
   or vegetable broth

1 cup dry white wine

Salt and freshly ground pepper

½ teaspoon dry thyme

½ cup grated Parmesan cheese

1 Melt butter in a heavy, good-size saucepan. Add onions and squash. Sauté lightly over low-medium heat until onions begin to wilt.

2 Add rice and mushrooms. Stir continuously 1 or 2 minutes or until rice is well-coated with sauce. Gradually add boiling water or broth as you stir. Add wine, salt and pepper to taste, and thyme. Continue stirring.

3 When rice has absorbed all the liquid, add grated cheese and stir vigorously until it's incorporated into the rice. Serve hot. Place additional grated cheese at the table for individual use.

TODAY I'm writing in the monastery kitchen as I listen to Yehudi Menuhin's poignant rendition of Bach sonatas and partitas for solo cello. I feel sheltered from today's nasty weather—rain and the first hail of the season. It's cold and damp, and the wind seems to scurry across the property. I mentally calculate how much wood we'll need for the rest of the day and the entire night. The last few days were unusually warm, so a fire wasn't necessary and therefore I didn't bother to pile up wood indoors. Today I must compensate for that small negligence.

The truth is, I was busy planting the last tulip bulbs around the Lourdes grotto. Next spring, God willing, Our Lady and Saint Bernadette will be surrounded and kindly saluted by these gracious flowers planted in their honor. Later in the season, lively perennials will replace the tulips. It's always indeed a joy to plan a small garden like this. It's a much-needed improvement for that particular side of the garden; at the same time, it expresses our loving devotion to the Mother of God.

During these mid November days surrounding the feast of Saint Martin, I'm keenly reminded that in the south of France the wine growers have begun to taste the result of their labors. This well-established tradition began when Saint Martin imported and planted the first vineyards around Tours on the Loire Valley. He and Saint Vincent thus became the patron saints of winemakers. Many French folk sayings (*dictons*) allude to the intimate connection between Saint Martin and wine.

A strong link has always existed between monks and wine. During the Middle Ages, monks developed the wine industry that is still going strong. Most Christian monks believe wine has an almost sacred and mystical element to it. Psalm 104:15 tells us wine gladdens human hearts. Drunk in moderation, wine remains a daily staple in the diet of most French and Mediterranean monasteries.

> *A bittersweet autumn doesn't plunge dramatically into the chilly vortex of winter; it evolves imperceptibly, weather, mood, and menu, while simultaneously the appetite for comfort rises.*
>
> MOLLY O'NEILL

Saint Benedict, who was thoroughly ascetic but also a very wise and practical man, provided in his *Rule* that monks could include a half pint of wine in their daily diet. Half a pint is plenty to complement and balance the otherwise frugal monastic meal.

Most people think of wine primarily as a drink, but as a cook I also think of how to use it in the kitchen, especially with desserts. For instance, for Saint Martin's Day, I used a wonderful recipe from a friend in Paris, Anne Hudson, a food writer and radio host. A great talent in French cuisine, she loves to experiment with wine in her cooking. She came out with this wonderful recipe for pears cooked in Sauternes wine, appropriately called *poires pochees au Sauternes*.

POIRES POCHEES AU SAUTERNES
(Pears Cooked in Sauternes Wine)
8 SERVINGS

8 pears, firm and in good shape
1 bottle Sauternes wine
½ lemon, peeled
1 vanilla bean
8 scoops of vanilla ice cream
24 mint leaves

1 Peel pears with great care and leave intact. Sprinkle lemon juice over them.

2 Pour Sauternes wine into a cooking pot, add lemon peel and vanilla, and bring to a gentle boil.

3 As wine boils, carefully add pears, reduce heat to low–medium, and gently cook 8 to 10 minutes. Remove pears and cool.

4 Place pears on serving plates and pour a bit of wine over them. Top each pear with a scoop of ice cream. Add 2 or 3 whole fresh mint leaves to each serving. Serve immediately.

T'**VE WRITTEN** six cookbooks in twenty-seven years. *Twelve Months of Monastery Soups* took six years from the moment I started writing the recipes to publication day—a long time indeed in one's life journey as a cookbook writer.

Cookbook writing, for many, has become a profession. For others it is simply a hobby. Some cookbooks are creative and excel in the quality of their recipes; others champion everything new and fashionable. Fashions change so quickly in the United States, especially when it comes to food. France has a longer cooking tradition, so classical French cuisine (*la cuisine classique*) remains an antidote to what is often a passing fad. For a solid, reputable recipe, rely on the repertoire of the traditional cuisine. These recipes have been tested for several centuries and can easily be personalized for creativity's sake.

Some recent cookbooks love to show new techniques, new ingredients, new approaches to food. They're all about newness. To them I ask, what about substance? Is it enough to charm readers with new, well-structured, exotic recipes, or fewer calories? All of these are fine, but there is more to real cooking. The food writer must transmit a clear, distinctive message in the consistency of his or her recipes and in the consistency of his or her philosophy and approach to cooking.

Darkness and light divide the tall sky, the rumble of thunder passes over distant mountains. The evening is cool, and beyond the slackening rain, through broken clouds, a moon immaculate.

ISHIKAWA JOZAN

There is plenty of room for improvement and innovation in assembling recipes, but recipes must show an "inner consistency" that makes each plate unique. Many cookbooks published each year are more repetitious and similar than distinctive and uniquely creative. Editors sometimes base their decisions on what is a passing fad or on the fame of the author rather than on the quality and authenticity of the recipes.

Speaking of recipes, today's evening meal is *omelette au potiron*. It allows me to use fresh eggs from our few chickens (thank God they are still laying) and the seasonal produce available this late in the garden: leeks, parsley, and the recently harvested squash. A plain omelette may be simple and quick in its preparation, but oh what a delight to the palate. And omelettes are always light and nourishing.

OMELETTE AU POTIRON (Squash and Leek Omelette)

4–6 SERVINGS

Olive oil
1 medium-size butternut squash, peeled, seeded, and diced
2 leeks, cleaned and thinly sliced (white parts only)
8 eggs
6 tablespoons milk
Salt and freshly ground pepper
A few parsley sprigs, finely chopped

1 Pour olive oil into a large skillet. Add squash and leeks. Cook slowly over low-medium heat for 12 to 15 minutes. Stir frequently, cover between stirring. Add more oil if needed.

2 Break eggs into a deep bowl. Add milk, salt, and pepper, and beat thoroughly. Add squash and leeks to egg mixture and mix well.

3 Raise heat to medium and place empty skillet on heat (add oil if necessary). Pour egg-vegetable mixture into skillet and distribute evenly. Cover skillet. After 2 or 3 minutes, lower heat to low-medium.

4 When omelette seems almost done, use spatula to loosen it underneath, and then flip omelette onto a large plate or platter. Gently slide reverse side of omelette back into skillet. Cover skillet and cook for about 2 minutes.

5 Slice omelette into 4 or 6 even portions and place on warm serving plates. Top with fresh, finely chopped parsley and serve immediately.

Thanksgiving Day

THANKSGIVING arrives on the fourth Thursday in November as autumn slowly winds down and seeks to merge into winter. Autumn is a time to express and spread gratitude across the Earth, the nation, the world. The miracles of abundance harvested in the fall started early in the spring, as the soil received the seed, which was nurtured by the rays of the sun and the rain from the heavens. Now, as we relive the harvest miracle once again, Mother Earth renders fabulous returns. Our bushel baskets overflow, giving clear evidence of the blessings of abundance.

As I move around the kitchen doing the daily chores, I reflect on the meaning of today's celebration. Thanksgiving and gratefulness are thoroughly monastic inner attitudes. Since monks are entirely dependent on the providence of a loving Father, I have so much to be thankful for in all I receive from him daily:

I **AM THANKFUL** for the sun, the moon, and the rain that made our garden grow and in turn produced an abundant harvest.

I **AM THANKFUL** for the daily sunsets at the time of Vespers, for those last rays of the sun filled the world with undying beauty and my soul with serenity.

I **AM THANKFUL** for the daylight that gives me ample time to do my tasks.

I **AM THANKFUL** for my parents, family, friends, neighbors, and helpers and for all loved ones far and near. Everyone is remembered daily in prayer, especially at the close of the day.

I **AM THANKFUL** for the gift of good health, which allows me to continue working day by day, singing the Lord's praises.

I **AM THANKFUL** for so many things that there isn't room to mention them all. I'll simply say that every moment and occasion of the day gives me something or someone to be grateful for.

Be filled with the Spirit, as you sing psalms and hymns and spiritual songs among yourselves, singing and making melody to the Lord in your hearts, giving thanks to God the Father at all times.

EPHESIANS 5:18-20

Today one of my kitchen chores is peeling and cubing the large pumpkins we recently harvested. Our special dessert for today is a pumpkin tart. Thanksgiving is a time to enjoy tantalizing pumpkin, mince, and other pies. Their rich taste and crunchy texture add the final touch to the day's convivial dinner. Here is today's recipe of *tarte de potiron*. The dough is extra special, a more festive and elaborate one in honor of the occasion.

TARTE AU POTIRON (French Pumpkin Pie)

6–8 SERVINGS

DOUGH
1 cup all-purpose flour
1 cup sugar
2½ ounces butter, cubed
⅓ cup ice water
⅓ cup walnuts, finely chopped
½ teaspoon salt
4 tablespoons sour cream

FILLING
1 butternut squash or ⅓ hubbard
   (winter) squash or pumpkin,
   peeled, seeded, and cubed
½ bottle Marsala wine
¾ cup sugar
8 tablespoons honey
1 lemon rind, grated
1 orange rind, grated
2 eggs, beaten
3 tablespoons milk

1 In a food processor combine flour, sugar, and butter. Mix briefly until mixture resembles coarse cornmeal. Add water, chopped walnuts, salt, and sour cream, then mix until a dough is formed. Work dough gently for 1 or 2 minutes, refrigerate at least 2 hours, then knead.

2 Place squash cubes in a deep pan, add Marsala wine, sugar, honey, and grated lemon and orange rinds and cook until squash is done. Let cool.

3 Place eggs and milk in a blender and whirl. Add squash mixture to blender and whirl until even.

4 Preheat oven to 350° F. Roll out dough on a floured surface until you have a circle that is roughly 2 inches larger in diameter than the circumference of your tart pan. Thoroughly butter the tart pan and lay dough circle in it. Trim edges in a decorative fashion.

5 Pour egg–squash mixture into tart pan, filling it to ½ inch from the top. Bake about 30 minutes or until tart is golden brown. Cool slightly. Slice into even wedges and serve at room temperature.

RECENTLY I was asked by a food writer how I go about composing new recipes. I told her I always try to use five basic principles:

SEASONAL Throughout the centuries, monastic fare has basically been seasonal, depending mainly on the fresh produce of our gardens and orchards. The monk's daily schedule, work, and worship are marked by the cycle of the seasons. In his daily life, the monk seeks to integrate the harmonious interactions among the rhythms of the seasons, the rhythms of the liturgy, and the rhythms of the heart. In many ways, this is what the mystery of monastic life is all about.

MONASTIC Known for its simplicity, sobriety, wholesomeness, and basic good taste, our monastic diet is mostly based on products from our farm, gardens, and orchards, and the dishes are presented with simplicity and basic good taste, but monastic fare is more than just plain, ordinary, good food. Though marked by frugality and simplicity, monastic cooking relies a great deal on the freshness and healthiness of the products, on the wisdom of local tradition, and on the common sense, spirituality, and resourcefulness of the monk chef's imagination. Monastic fare doesn't lack its own chic elegance, for simplicity itself is synonymous with elegance (and a good dose of spirituality is sometimes the best spice).

BASICALLY VEGETARIAN Vegetables play an important role in monastic cooking. The monastic diet has remained, throughout the course of the centuries, essentially vegetarian. Cheese, milk, eggs, and seafood are allowed in the monastic diet and thus often become the basis of my recipes.

HEALTHY I often strive to combine elements that enhance good health, sound nutrition, and basic good taste. When well prepared and attractively presented in courses according to the traditional pattern of a French meal, a simple meal can become a wonderful occasion for celebration. Monastic kitchens, the inspiration for my recipes, are arranged with a great deal of efficiency and industry to allow the creation of wholesome food of unique quality.

*I believe in the sun
even when
it's not shining.
I believe in love
even when
feeling it not.
I believe in God
even when
He is silent.*

ANCIENT JEWISH SAYING

FRENCH In general, my recipes don't represent the gastronomical world of classical French cooking. They reflect more the family and country style of French cooking with which I was raised. This sort of cooking is earthy, honest, simple, and always pleasant to the palate. French cuisine continues to evolve, with new techniques and methods of preparation continually being developed. I'm hopeful that new seasonings and experimental ways of cooking will lead to the sort of cuisine that continues to exalt the value of fine taste while remaining consistent with the traditional classical cooking of France, in which the result is exquisite to both the eyes and the palate.

PURÉE DI POTIRON ET RICOTTA (Quick Squash and Ricotta Purée)

6 SERVINGS

1 medium-size hubbard (winter) squash, peeled, seeded, and cut into lengthwise pieces
7 tablespoons olive oil
4 medium-size white onions, peeled and finely chopped
1 large-size carrot, peeled and thinly sliced
½ cup dry white wine
12 ounces of fresh ricotta cheese
Salt and nutmeg
6 tablespoons
    Parmesan-Reggiano cheese
Butter

1 Preheat oven to 350° F. Place squash slices on a flat aluminum tray and bake for about 30 minutes. Remove from heat and set aside to cool, then mash with a masher. Reduce oven temperature to 300° F.

2 Pour olive oil into a skillet and lightly sauté onions and carrots over low–medium heat about 2 minutes. Add wine, raise heat to medium, and continue stirring 8 to 10 minutes.

3 Pour mixture into a large bowl or casserole. Mash mixture. Add mashed squash, cheeses, and salt and nutmeg to taste. Mix thoroughly. Butter a deep, long baking dish. Pour squash–ricotta mixture into dish and distribute evenly. Place dish in oven and bake 25 to 30 minutes at 300° F. Serve hot.

AS WE REACH the end of November, the darkness of the approaching winter seems to surround us from all sides. Country folks know the freezing cold is soon to arrive and stay. The snow invariably arrives around Thanksgiving, or more precisely around November 30, the Feast of Saint Andrew.

Toward the end of November, as the first Sunday of Advent makes its yearly appearance, I continue preparing the Christmas gifts begun in October. I already have a number of jams, pickles, and relishes prepared. With Thanksgiving behind us and December at our doorstep, I'm now concentrating on chutneys, vinegars, salsas, and tapenade.

I particularly enjoy surprising people with homemade tapenade, a concoction quintessentially Provençal that's not often found in the American supermarkets. A well-concocted tapenade has the aroma and taste one associates with the lovely and sunny land of Provence, France. Besides, tapenade has multiple uses. It can be served as a spread on baguettes or crackers, or it can be used as a filling for hard-boiled eggs, tomatoes, and avocados. The Provençal people love to spread it on fresh *pain de campagne*, "country bread."

TAPENADE

YIELD: 6 OR 8 4-OUNCE CONTAINERS

16 ounces pitted black olives
½ cup capers
1 cup olive oil
6 teaspoons lemon juice
6 garlic cloves, minced
2 tablespoons Dijon mustard
2 tablespoons dried thyme, rosemary, basil, bay leaf
Freshly ground pepper

1 Chop olives and garlic and place them in a food processor or blender. Add capers, olive oil, lemon juice, mustard, herbs, and pepper. (No salt is needed because the olives are salty).

2 Blend mixture until thoroughly smooth. Add more olive oil if necessary and check seasonings. After blending, mixture must have the consistency of smooth butter.

3 Place tapenade in small 4-ounce plastic containers and refrigerate until you need them. To avoid having to refrigerate them, sterilize small 4-ounce canning jars and fill them with tapenade to the top. Put the lids on and place them in boiling water for about 15 minutes to seal them.

DECEMBER

*And after him
came the chill
December;
Yet he through
merry feasting
which he made,
and great bonfires,
did not the cold
remember
His Saviour's birth
his mind so much
did glad.*

EDMUND SPENSER

THE EXUBERANT FIRE from our wood-burning stove throws comfortable heat throughout the entire kitchen as gentle smoke escapes slowly through the chimney pipe. It's no surprise that December has been nicknamed "Smoky" by some writers because of the abundant smoke visibly emerging from chimneys all across the countryside, including our own.

December is usually a month of extremely cold temperatures in the northeastern United States. It's the month of wind, frost, and snowstorms. It's also the darkest month of the year: By 4:00 PM the long winter night begins, and it takes resilience and creativity to put up with the extended dark hours.

The cozy kitchen inspires endless creativity. While listening to Bach's beautiful Advent cantata, I continue preparing and preserving food that later will be used as small Christmas gifts for many of our kind and generous monastery friends and for our annual monastic craft fair. When I think of the treasure of friendship and how much each friend means to me, I enjoy preparing food far ahead of time that will delight our many friends' palates.

Every day I organize my time in the kitchen because I need to prepare as much food as possible in advance. As Advent progresses, more time will be needed for prayer, for the chant, and for putting up Christmas decorations. Now is the time to complete the food preserves and get an early start on some pre-Christmas baking.

Since we still have pumpkins, apples, and pears from Thanksgiving, today's kitchen activities are concentrated on chutney preparations. Our chutneys are always popular at the craft fair and among our friends, especially those with English and Irish backgrounds. For them, chutney is a staple often served at the table.

As I slowly add the spices to the chutney sauce, the kitchen seems intoxicated with the perfumes and aromas springing forth from the large iron pot. From time to time I stir it and add a bit more vinegar to be sure it doesn't burn. The mystery of chutney is that all sorts of mixtures and combinations are possible. All you need is an artful imagination.

PUMPKIN-APPLE-PEAR CHUTNEY

10 PINTS

10 tart apples, peeled and chopped
4 pears, peeled and chopped
1 small-size pumpkin, peeled, seeded, cut in chunks, cooked, and mashed
2 onions, diced
2 red peppers, diced
2½ cups brown sugar
2 teaspoons cumin
2 teaspoons allspice
3 tablespoons mustard seed
2 tablespoons ginger
3 hot red peppers, chopped
2 teaspoons salt
3 cloves of garlic, minced
1 quart cider vinegar

1 Place ingredients in a large saucepan. Simmer until thick, for about 1 hour. As mixture thickens, stir often so it doesn't stick. Pour mixture into hot jars to ¼ inch from the top.

2 Put lids on jars and seal them by placing them in boiling water (covering the tops of the jars) for at least 20 minutes. Make sure tops are thoroughly sealed.

NOTE: TO MAKE CHUTNEY SPICIER, INCREASE THE AMOUNT OF HOT PEPPERS, MUSTARD, AND/OR GINGER. ALTERNATIVELY, THE DISH WILL BE MILDER IF YOU REMOVE THE SEEDS FROM THE HOT PEPPER.

AS WE UNDERTAKE our yearly Advent journey, we feel instinctively drawn to the Divine Presence, to he who helps us on our journey by driving away the negative elements that fill daily life: fear, despair, depression, insecurity, instability, suspicion.

Advent is a time of preparation and expectation. It's a symbol of his final coming in glory at the end of times. While Advent gives us an opportunity to be joyous in the promise of the Lord's coming, it also teaches us to abide by the wisdom of sobriety and frugality in our ordinary lives. Being guided by a sense of sobriety and temperance in our approach to food during our Advent days doesn't imply a rejection of good food or good taste, which after all are gifts from the Lord. What it means, at least from a monastic point of view, is not to overindulge or abuse the gifts by overeating and overdrinking. The goal remains the same: Through simplicity and sobriety, observe the proper use of God's gifts daily and enjoy them in moderation.

The beginning of Advent is also the time we become deeply reacquainted with the physical realities of winter: the cold, the sleet, the snow, the darkness, and in particular the long, somber nights. Dusk descends upon us at a surprisingly early time. It's as if the harsh reality of winter is there to tell us that part of the Advent journey involves traveling from the forces of darkness and sin into the radiance of God's light, from which hope and grace shine forth.

My kitchen abilities are very much marked by this winter cyclical rhythm. After the heavy frosts of the last couple of days, I work to salvage what is left in the garden: leeks, cabbages, Swiss chard, beets, turnips, carrots, parsley, and the last of the salad greens. These last have survived until now because I've been covering them with heavy plastic at night to protect them from the frost. But all good things come to an end, including the fresh produce from our gardens. Tonight I'll prepare, probably for the last time this year, a salad from our own fresh produce.

In keeping with the theme of Advent sobriety, tonight's meal will be a basic creamy soup made from our garden potatoes, leeks, carrots, and turnips followed by a fresh salad from our last greens and beets with hard-boiled eggs. A basic meal such as that, full of monastic simplicity and good taste, not only satisfies the body's hunger but also the soul's. After consuming such a meal, one is replenished but still feels light as a feather. The delights of the table are adhered to with the consciousness that we are also spiritual beings and that our spirituality must never be neglected.

Long is our winter
Dark is our night
Come, set us free
O saving light.

15TH-CENTURY HYMN

POTAGE BERRICHONNE (Berrichonne Soup)

6 – 8 SERVINGS

10 cups water
6 potatoes, peeled and cubed
3 leeks, washed and thinly sliced
   (white parts only)
2 medium-size carrots,
   peeled and cubed
2 medium-size turnips,
   washed and cubed
4 parsley sprigs, finely chopped
Salt and pepper

GARNISH
2 teaspoons butter
5 slices of bread, cubed
   (9 cubes per slice)

1 Bring water to a quick boil. Reduce heat to medium and add vegetables, parsley, salt, and pepper. Cover pot and cook slowly, between 25 and 30 minutes (add more water if needed).

2 After 30 minutes, turn off heat. With pot covered, let it rest for about 15 minutes. Afterward, blend soup in a blender until it's creamy and even.

3 Melt butter in a frying pan. Add bread cubes, turning them often until all sides are equally browned. Set them aside until ready to serve.

4 Reheat soup and serve hot. Garnish each serving with 5 or 6 croutons.

SALADE CAMPAGNARDE (Country-Style Salad)

6 SERVINGS

1 bunch fresh salad greens
   (arugula, romaine lettuce,
   or whatever is available)
3 fresh medium beets, peeled,
   halved, and then thinly sliced
2 apples, peeled and thinly sliced
1 small red onion, peeled and
   thinly sliced
6 eggs (one per person),
   hard-boiled and halved

VINAIGRETTE
7 tablespoons olive oil
3 tablespoons red-wine vinegar
1 teaspoon French mustard
Salt and freshly ground pepper

1 Wash and dry salad greens and place them in a salad bowl.

2 Boil beets 6 to 7 minutes. Rinse under cold water and drain. After 5 minutes, add beets, apples, and onion to salad greens. Toss lightly.

3 Place 2 egg halves on each serving plate.

4 Prepare and blend vinaigrette well. Pour over salad and toss evenly. Place salad next to eggs on serving plates. Serve at room temperature.

DECEMBER 6 ✦ Saint Nicholas Day

*A*S OUR DAYS continue to shorten and winter sets in, the limited amount of daylight assumes a considerable significance. Early in the morning, after the Offices and breakfast, I hasten to feed and water our farm animals and then return promptly to the kitchen to start an honest day's work.

Today, on Saint Nicholas Day, I'll follow the old monastic custom of baking bread for the holidays. Monks usually bake bread in sufficient quantity for the needs of the monastery and its guests as well as for gift-giving to friends and benefactors. The sharing of loaves of freshly baked breads on the occasion of the Lord's birth is an experience of deep joy. Bread, after all, is intimately connected to the person of Christ, who left us the gift of his body under the species of bread.

As we slowly move toward Christmas, many varieties of bread are baked in the monastery kitchen: brown bread flavored with honey or molasses, regular white bread, and more festive loaves enhanced by grains, nuts, and dried fruit. The breads will be wrapped and placed in the freezer or a cold storage room until Christmas Day, when we will lovingly give them as gifts.

This old monastic tradition is being assimilated by others in the secular world. More and more people, especially in the countryside, find great joy in offering a loaf of fresh bread as an infinitely personal and meaningful gift.

This recipe takes its name from the Christmas saint, Nicholas, whom many tend to identify with the legend of Santa Claus. (Poor, dear Saint Nicholas, what have they done to you?)

The feast of Saint Nicholas is usually the least cold of December days, Except when it snows on that day, then winter is certainly here.

EARLY FRENCH SAYING

SAINT NICHOLAS BREAD

2 LOAVES

3 packages active dry yeast
2 tablespoons brown sugar
1 cup lukewarm water
6 cups white wheat flour
5 cups all-purpose white flour
6 teaspoons salt
5 cups milk, heated and
    allowed to cool
1 cup dried raisins
8 tablespoons molasses
    (or honey)
2 eggs, beaten

1 Butter or grease two 12-inch bread pans. Set them aside.

2 Put lukewarm water, sugar, and yeast in a deep bowl. Stir to dissolve sugar and yeast. Allow mixture to stand 6 to 8 minutes.

3 In a large casserole, combine the whole wheat and white flour. Add salt, milk, raisins, molasses (or honey), and yeast mixture. Blend ingredients well until liquid is absorbed by flour. Work ingredients into a dough, then place it on a flat, floured surface or table.

4 Knead dough for at least 15 minutes or until dough becomes smooth. From time to time, sprinkle dough with extra flour to keep it from sticking to work surface.

5 Place dough in a good-size, well-buttered casserole or bowl. Cover dough with a wet towel and allow it to rise for about two hours or until it doubles in size.

6 Punch dough at the center, cover again with the wet towel, and let it rise until it doubles in size.

7 Move dough from casserole or bowl onto flat surface or table. Press it flat. Divide dough into two equal parts. Roll each part into cylinder shape and set them in two well-greased bread pans. Use your fingers to tuck the ends under and spread dough evenly in pan, shaping loaf a bit higher at the center. Use a knife to cut a cross into the top of the bread.

8 Brush loaf tops with beaten egg. Cover loaves with the wet towel and let rise until they double in size.

9 Preheat oven to 375° F.

10 Brush the loaf tops with beaten eggs, and place the pans in the oven. Bake for 45 minutes or until the tops turn deep brown. Remove loaves from pans and let cool on a wire rack.

ADVENT is a constant reminder of the coming of God in our midst. Awareness of the approaching coming of Christ, as our Lord and Savior gives Advent its unique perspective and character. We know Christ came more than two thousand years ago, but the grace of Advent is to also bring forth the awareness of Christ's presence among us *today*.

Our contemplative Advent days, though quiet and calm, nonetheless contain a certain amount of fuss and busyness, especially in the monastery kitchen, the hub of endless activities in preparation for the forthcoming feast.

As Christmas gets closer, the making of edible gifts continues in earnest. Homemade gifts may lack the elegance and allure of those made commercially, but they contain the simplicity, gaiety, and warmth of the human touch. Gifts made by friendly hands are usually the best presents one receives.

Today I happen to be deeply involved in the preparation of brownies and cookies. A box of moist brownies is a treat any time of the year, but especially during the holidays. Today is the Feast of Our Lady of Guadalupe, so I decided to name the Guadalupe-brownies recipe in honor of the humble maiden chosen to become the Mother of God. The original recipe is from a friend who says she's "addicted" to brownies and a true chocolate connoisseur. Throughout the years, I have modified the recipe here and there, especially as to the liqueur flavors. This is the latest rendition.

People, look East,

the time is near

of the crowning

of the year.

Make your house

fair as you are able,

Trim the hearth

and set the table.

People, look East

and sing today,

Christ, the Lord,

is on the way.

ANCIENT FRENCH CAROL

GUADALUPE BROWNIES

16 SQUARES

3 ounces unsweetened chocolate,
   chopped into small pieces
1 stick sweet butter,
   sliced into small pieces
2 large eggs
1 cup raw sugar (natural cane)
5 tablespoons Grand Marnier liqueur
1 cup all-purpose flour
¼ teaspoon baking powder
Pinch of salt
½ cup pine nuts, toasted

1 Preheat oven to 325° F. Thoroughly butter and flour an 8-inch square baking pan. Discard excess flour.

2 Use a double boiler, with water boiling lightly, to melt chocolate and butter. Stir continuously until mixture is smooth and even. Remove the top boiler and allow it to cool.

3 Use a large bowl to beat eggs and sugar with a mixer until mixture thickens. Add chocolate mixture and Grand Marnier and continue beating.

4 Sift flour into a separate bowl. Add baking powder and salt and blend well. Add this mixture to egg-chocolate mixture and continue beating. Blend evenly.

5 Evenly spread batter in pan. Sprinkle evenly with pine nuts.

6 Place baking sheet in the center of the oven. Bake 35 to 40 minutes. Test brownies after 30 minutes by piercing the center with a knife. When the knife comes out clean, brownies are done.

7 Allow brownies to cool thoroughly before cutting into 16 even squares. Layer brownies between sheets of wax paper in airtight boxes and keep in a cool room. Brownies usually keep for a week or two, but they're best when made only 1 week ahead of time.

T'S MID DECEMBER, late Advent. Each morning during *lectio divina,* the reading of the ancient prophecies from the Old Testament fills our hearts with longing and expectation. There is such a majestic and poetic richness in the expressions used by the prophets. I never tire of hearing them proclaimed in our small, austere chapel, or simply reading them in the solitude of the monastic cell. The prophets are my companions on the road to Bethlehem. Their words nurture my prayer and refresh my tired spirit. Again and again, as I do with the psalms, I frequently turn to them for solace, for inspiration, for strength, and for hope to press onward.

One of Advent's memorable moments is the day I begin baking Christmas cookies. First, the flurry of preparation that precedes baking. I empty the kitchen, then assemble the recipes and ingredients. Today, in spite of the beautiful clear and sunny light, it's a cold frosty day, and the heat of the wood-burning stove is soothing and inspiring as I gather the energy for three or four hours of steady baking. Bach's Advent Cantatas lift my heart to prayer and complete the picture.

Cookie-making, like bread-making, is a mainstay in many monasteries. The French monasteries call it *faire les biscuits.* The notable differences between European and American cookies mostly involve the amount of butter and other ingredients. I usually experiment with both and end up with a concoction that's something in between.

Whatever the result, homemade cookies make wonderful gifts for friends, families, and children. We sort them by color and size and carefully place them

It will be said
on that day,
Lo, this is our God;
we have waited
for him, so that
he might save us.
This is the LORD
for whom
we have waited;
let us be glad
and rejoice in
his salvation.

ISAIAH 25:6–9

in imported tin boxes we save throughout the year. The boxes are stored in a dry corner of the basement. A few days before Christmas, we wrap each tin, tie a ribbon around it, and attach a gift card.

Throughout the years I've experimented with cookie recipes, some from Europe and others shared with me by friends. These are a few of my favorites. They all bear the names of Advent and Christmas saints. The first recipe is from Belgium, where the cookies are called Saint Klauss cookies after Saint Nicholas, whose feast is celebrated December 6.

SAINT NICHOLAS COOKIES

3 DOZEN COOKIES

⅔ cup sweet butter
½ cup brown sugar
1¼ cups all-purpose flour
1½ teaspoons ground cinnamon
¼ teaspoon ground anise
Pinch of ground ginger
Pinch of ground nutmeg
¼ teaspoon double-acting
   baking powder
1 tablespoon vanilla extract
Pinch of salt
2 tablespoons milk
1 cup sliced almonds

1 Cream butter and sugar together until very light in color. Beat in the milk and set mixture aside.

2 Sift flour, cinnamon, anise, ginger, nutmeg, baking powder, salt, and vanilla together and stir into butter mixture. Wrap cookie dough in wax paper and refrigerate for 1 hour.

3 Preheat oven to 350° F. Roll cookie dough into a 1/16-inch-thick rectangle. Cut dough into 1½-inch by 2½-inch rectangles, then cut the cookies apart. Transfer cookies to a lightly buttered baking sheet, brush tops with milk, and gently press sliced almonds into cookies.

4 Bake on center rack for 10 to 12 minutes or until cookies are firm to the touch.

ANGEL GABRIEL BUTTER COOKIES

3 DOZEN COOKIES

1¼ cups unbleached, all-purpose flour
½ teaspoon baking powder
1/8 teaspoon salt
8 tablespoons sweet butter, softened
1 cup granulated or brown sugar
1 large egg
½ teaspoon vanilla extract

1 Combine flour, baking powder, and salt in a medium bowl. Mix well and set aside.

2 Beat butter with an electric mixer on medium speed. Gradually add sugar, beating until mixture is light and fluffy. Beat in egg and vanilla, then reduce speed and add flour mixture, mixing just until they're combined. Divide dough into four equal portions and wrap in plastic. Refrigerate until firm, about 1 hour.

3 Preheat oven to 325° F. Roll out one portion of dough on a floured surface, cut into desired shapes, and arrange about 1 inch apart on buttered nonstick baking sheets. Decorate as desired.

4 Bake for about 5 minutes. Rotate baking sheets, then continue baking about 5 minutes or until cookies are golden. Transfer cookies to a wire rack and allow to cool. Repeat process until all dough has been used. Finish decorating and serve.

Saint Joseph cookies originated in German monasteries, where they're a perennial favorite among German monks and nuns. Often they're placed in charming boxes and sold in the monastery boutiques just before Christmas.

SAINT JOSEPH COOKIES

3 DOZEN COOKIES

2 tablespoons butter, softened

2 tablespoons and
   2½ cups all-purpose flour

¾ teaspoon baking powder

½ teaspoon ground cloves

1 teaspoon ground cinnamon

¼ teaspoon ground nutmeg

1 cup unblanched almonds, ground

2 tablespoons candied citron,
   finely chopped

2 tablespoons candied lemon,
   finely chopped

2 tablespoons candied orange,
   finely chopped

2 eggs

½ cup granulated sugar

½ cup honey

½ cup milk

EGG-WASH GLAZE

1 egg white

½ tablespoon water

SUGAR GLAZE

1 cup confectioners'
   (powdered) sugar

6 tablespoons milk

1 Butter a 17½-inch by 11½-inch jellyroll pan with softened butter. Sprinkle the pan with 2 tablespoons of flour, tilting pan from side to side to coat it evenly. Discard excess flour.

2 Preheat oven to 400° F. Sift remaining flour, baking powder, cloves, cinnamon, and nutmeg into a large bowl. Add almonds and candied fruits. Set aside.

3 Beat eggs and sugar until thick and very light in color. Stir in flour mixture, honey, and milk. Continue stirring until well blended. Spread evenly in pan.

4 If you plan to use a sugar glaze, skip to Step 5. If you prefer to use an egg-wash glaze, mix an egg white with water. Brush mixture onto dough.

5 Bake cookie on the center rack for 12 minutes or until cookie is firm to the touch.

6 With two large serving spatulas or turners, lift cookie out of pan and place on a wire rack. If you're using a sugar glaze, mix confectioners' (powdered) sugar and milk. Brush glaze on the cookie while it's still warm. Let glaze set 3 to 4 minutes, then transfer cookie to a flat surface and cut into 2½-inch by 1½-inch rectangles. If you wish to use cookie cutters and/or apply icing in special patterns, let cookie cool for a few minutes, then cut cookies and apply icing with a watercolor brush.

Unto us a child is born!
King of all creation,
Came he to
a world forlorn,
the Lord
of every nation.
Cradled in
a stall was he
With sleepy cows
and asses;
But the very
beasts could see
That he
all men surpasses.
Now may Mary's son,
who came
So long ago to love us,
Lead us all
with hearts aflame
Unto the joys
above us.

15TH CENTURY CAROL

EVERY COUNTRY, every monastery, every household has its own traditions and ways of celebrating the birthday of the Savior. Some celebrations include lavish decorations, fancy ornaments, sumptuous meals, and expensive drinks. I have a problem with such an approach to Christmas because it deviates from the original Christmas message: the reality of Christ's humble birth in a Bethlehem cave, surrounded not by luxury but by simple shepherds and animals.

Our Christmas celebrations, though "festive" in a monastic context, are tempered by monastic frugality. We rejoice and honor the Lord's birthday with joyful celebrations that include a convivial special dinner at the monastic table. The menu may include exquisite and flavorful dishes, but we're keenly conscious of not departing too far from our basic monastic simplicity and from the thought that many poor people around the world lack even the most basic Christmas repast. It's incumbent upon us as Christians to always remember the plight of the poor, the homeless, and the hungry, for in them the Lord Christ still manifests himself to us. Thus, when we plan our Christmas menu we seek to create an appetizing meal that combines festivity with restraint.

The Son of Man, the Gospel tells us, came eating and drinking, and throughout his life he attached particular importance to his meals. He enjoyed eating meals with his disciples and the meal prepared in Bethany by that marvelous disciple and hostess Martha. And it's not too presumptuous to think he immensely enjoyed the meals he shared with his mother, Mary, and his foster father, the good Saint Joseph. During his public life, Jesus didn't hesitate to multiply loaves and fishes to attend to the needs of the starving crowds. These Gospel episodes remind us of Jesus' involvement with food and show us how truly human he was.

At the end of his life, Christ reminded us of the importance of food and drink by transforming plain bread and wine into his Body and Blood, leaving both as nourishment for our souls. In the Gospel context, food is a mark of Christ's love for every one of his creatures.

It's impossible to arrive at any Christian concept of food spirituality without first grasping the implications of the mystery of the Incarnation. Our Christmas meal is a humble reminder of these truths. As Christians we eat, drink, and rejoice today because Jesus, in becoming human, became one of us. He came to teach us how to live. Part of this teaching includes learning to eat, drink, and share food and to be thankful to our Father for the generosity of his gifts.

The point of departure for our monastic Christmas menu is our own tradition, which provides a wonderful wealth of resources. Tradition, especially a culinary one, allows us to feel connected to those who preceded us and to those who will come after us. As I search for inspiration among our many traditionally festive recipes, I see some that merit repeating.

Here is a sample Christmas menu at our monastery. From year to year I may exchange one recipe for another, for as much as I treasure tradition in the kitchen, it should never be used as an excuse to not try new things.

As usual, the monastic menu starts with a soup. Because it's Christmas Day, the soup is a bit more refined, more festive.

First course
CHRISTMAS POTAGE
6–8 SERVINGS

4 quarts water
1 large cauliflower head, trimmed
3 leeks, trimmed
4 potatoes
Pinch of salt
2 cups milk
2 eggs
White pepper

OPTIONAL: 2 TEASPOONS BUTTER, ⅓ CUP CHERVIL, FINELY CHOPPED

1 Place water in a large soup kettle.

2 Wash, peel, and slice vegetables into small pieces. Bring water to a boil and add vegetables and salt. Cover kettle and cook soup over medium heat about 20 minutes. Reduce heat to medium-low, cover, and allow to simmer 20 minutes. Stir from time to time.

3 Allow soup to cool, then whirl in a blender until even and creamy. Put soup back into the kettle and reheat at low–medium heat.

4 Place milk, eggs, and pepper to taste in blender and whirl thoroughly. Gradually add this mixture to soup and blend well. Continue cooking for 5 minutes or until ready to serve.

5 Just before serving, add 2 teaspoons of butter to soup (optional) and mix well. Pour soup into hot bowls and sprinkle with finely chopped chervil. Serve hot.

Second course

CREPES AUX EPINARDS (Crepes With Spinach Filling)

For crepe recipe, see page 60

6 SERVINGS

1 pound fresh spinach,
    soaked and chopped
4 hard-boiled eggs, chopped
1 onion, chopped
1 cup grated cheese
Butter
Salt and pepper

1 Prepare crepes according to recipe on page 60.

2 In a nonaluminum pan, melt butter and gently sauté onion. Add boiled and chopped spinach. Cook for 1 or 2 minutes. Turn off heat. Add chopped hard-boiled eggs, grated cheese, and salt and pepper to taste. Blend well.

3 Preheat oven to 300° F. Generously butter a large baking dish. Fill each crepe with a few spoonfuls of spinach mixture, roll up the crepe, and place it carefully in the baking dish. Repeat for rest of crepes. Cover crepes with heavy cream and bake for 15 to 20 minutes. Serve hot.

PURÉE OF CELERY ROOT AND VEGETABLES

6–8 SERVINGS

Water
2 large celery roots, peeled and
    cut into ¼-inch cubes
9 large potatoes, peeled and halved
Pinch of salt
2 tablespoons virgin olive oil
5 tablespoons unsalted butter
1 cup regular milk
Salt and freshly ground pepper

1 Pour water into a large casserole dish. Add celery-root cubes, potatoes, and salt. Boil over medium heat about 30 minutes or until vegetables are cooked. Drain thoroughly.

2 Pour olive oil into a small casserole dish and add butter and milk. Stir over low–medium heat until mixture turns warm and even.

3 Mash vegetables evenly or put them through a food mill. Place vegetables into large casserole dish and add butter-milk mixture and salt and pepper to taste. Blend well. Serve hot.

Third course

SALADE MELANGEE (Festive Mixed Salad)

6–8 SERVINGS

1 head Boston lettuce
1 head Bibb or leaf lettuce
1 medium radicchio
4 medium endives
1 bunch arugula
1 bunch watercress
Salt and pepper

OPTIONAL: CHOPPED CHIVES AND CHERVIL

SIMPLE VINAIGRETTE
1 teaspoon salt
½ teaspoon freshly ground pepper
2 tablespoons wine vinegar
2 tablespoons olive oil

1 Wash greens thoroughly and separate leaves. Do not cut or split leaves, only stems. Drain leaves completely, roll them in paper towels to keep them fresh and crisp. Refrigerate until ready to serve.

2 Just before serving, arrange greens in a salad bowl and mix. In a separate bowl, combine salt, pepper, and vinegar and stir thoroughly. Add oil and stir until ingredients are completely blended. Pour over greens and toss lightly. If you wish, sprinkle salad with finely chopped chives and/or chervil.

Fourth course

POIRES A LA BURGUIGNONE (Pears in Burgundy Wine)

6 SERVINGS

2 pounds small-size pears
1½ cups sugar
1 teaspoon cinnamon
1 cup water
1 cup red Burgundy wine

1 Peel pears, but keep them whole. Place them in a saucepan and add sugar, cinnamon, and water. Cover and bring to a light boil, usually about 10 minutes. Add wine and boil lightly 5 minutes. Simmer 15 minutes with saucepan uncovered.

2 Place pears in a shallow serving dish. Boil down juice until it is the consistency of a light syrup. Do not overboil. Pour juice over pears and chill. Must be served cold.

Index